Educational Reform
in New Mexico

Loyd S. Tireman

Educational Reform in New Mexico

Tireman, San José, and Nambé

David L. Bachelor

University of New Mexico Press
Albuquerque

First paperbound printing, 2010
New Mexico Paperbound ISBN: 978-0-8263-4950-7

15 14 13 12 11 10   1 2 3 4 5 6 7

Library of Congress Cataloging-in-Publication Data
Bachelor, David L.
Educational reform in New Mexico: Tireman, San José,
and Nambé
David L. Bachelor.—1st ed.
p.   cm.
Includes bibliographical references and index.
ISBN 0-8263-1276-4
1. Tireman, L. S. (Loyd Spencer), 1896–1959.
2. Educators—New Mexico—Biography.
3. San José Demonstration and Experimental School
(San José, Bernalillo County, N.M.)—History.
4. Nambé Community School (Nambe, N.M.)—History.
5. Education, Bilingual—New Mexico—History.
6. Intercultural education—New Mexico—History.
7. Education—New Mexico—Experimental methods—
History.
I. Title.
LB875.T732B33   1991
371'.03'0978961—dc20   91-2953

© 1991 by the University of New Mexico Press
All rights reserved.
First Edition

To
BJB
1934–1988

Contents

Preface / ix

Introduction / 3

Chapter 1 / 11
San José Demonstration and Experimental School:
The Beginning

Chapter 2 / 27
San José Demonstration and Experimental School:
The Program

Chapter 3 / 47
San José and New Mexico:
Teacher Training and Curriculum Revision

Chapter 4 / 63
Nambé Community School:
Origins and Community Health

Chapter 5 / 79
Nambé Community School:
Curriculum and Conservation

Chapter 6 / 105
An Assessment of Tireman's Work

Appendix / 119
The Mesaland Series

Notes / 129

Selected Bibliography / 151

Index / 163

Preface

A book such as this that has taken several years to prepare, has involved using original documents, and has been written under less than favorable conditions owes a great deal to many people. In more than the conventional sense the following pages are the result of a group effort. I wish to thank everyone who helped and to apologize to any person whose contribution is not explicitly mentioned below.

During the many months spent trying to reconstruct educational programs long ago ended and trying to piece together the elusive person of Loyd Tireman, one part of his genius became clear. Despite Tireman's public stance of hard-nosed empiricism, he was a wonderfully sensitive and intuitive judge of character. Without exception, the individuals hired by Tireman fifty years ago and more went on to have distinguished careers in education. They shared their experiences and recollections with me and proved that age does not have to dim enthusiasms nor confuse memories. This book could not have been completed without the gracious and unselfish help of Tireman's former colleagues at the experimental schools at San José and Nambé.

Contemporaries of Tireman, students and colleagues, who helped were: Del Baca Miera, Rudy Cordova, Harold Goff, Halene Weaver, Mela Sedillo Koebert, Maria Casias Vergara, Ann Jones, Laura Atkinson, Marguerite Johnson.

The original idea for this work grew out of Martin Berman's fine dissertation and subsequent conversations with him. Rita

Apodaca's research and dissertation greatly aided this book as well. The references to these two unpublished studies in the following chapters indicate how great a debt this book owes to the work of Berman and Apodaca.

Professor Albert W. Vogel was the original inspiration for the dissertations and this book. His knowledge of New Mexico history and fertile curiosity has motivated a whole generation of graduate students and junior faculty.

The descriptions of the experimental programs and the challenging times in which they occurred would not have been possible without the generous help of the late Professor Miles Zintz. Professor Frank Angel encouraged the research from the beginning and contributed many hours of valuable recollections and insights. Professor Angel's first job in education was at Nambé. He was able to look back over his long and distinguished career to lend the research a very valuable perspective.

A debt of gratitude is owed the following colleagues of mine for their help: Professor Zelda Maggart, Professor (and former Dean of the College of Education) Chester Travelstead, the late Professor T. M. Pearce, Professor Alexander Masley, Professor Guillermina Engelbrecht, Professor Sara Dawn Smith, Professor Phillip B. Gonzales.

Former Dean of the College of Education David Colton aided the research in many ways, and his support is gratefully acknowledged.

This investigation was assisted in innumerable ways by the fine staff at the Zimmerman Library and Special Collections Library at the University of New Mexico.

Sheila Coneen and David Johnson provided special help in advising the author about Tireman's health during his last years. This aid is gratefully acknowledged.

A special thanks is due the director and staff at the Rockefeller Archives Center. A grant from the center made possible the inspection of the records of the General Education Board for the years it was active in funding the San José School.

My colleagues in the department of Educational Foundations provided the intellectual atmosphere in which this book was written. For these exceptional people collegiality and intellectual support are much more than abstractions.

Finally, with deep appreciation, I acknowledge the loving encouragement of my friends Ann Nihlen and Cynthia Wolf.

Educational Reform in New Mexico

Introduction

Loyd Spencer Tireman was born in 1896 in Orchard, Iowa, and died in Albuquerque, New Mexico, in 1959. He came to the University of New Mexico in 1927 and, as a professor of elementary education, spent thirty-two years struggling with problems of teaching reading, bicultural education, and school-community relations. His calling was a strenuous, demanding one that resulted in limited recognition while he lived, and obscurity after he died.

In the year of his birth, agrarian radicalism, represented in Iowa by the Farmers' Alliance and the People's Party, was defeated at the polls by McKinley, Mark Hanna, and conservative financial interests.[1] But the disappointment in rural Iowa with the events on the national scene was offset by improving prices for farm goods. Loyd Tireman grew up in a period of sustained prosperity, though it was a time when people still remembered the difficult years. He was reared in an atmosphere of optimism based on hardy individualism and grass-roots democracy. The political and social environment of Tireman's youth was permeated by the Populist notion that the American system of government, though sometimes perverted by special interests, was the best system ever devised because it maximized opportunities for ambitious, enterprising individuals to get ahead.²

For Tireman's fellow Iowans, individual opportunity and democracy were synonymous, and education was the means for realizing both goals. Proper democratic education, furthermore, was locally controlled. The best education was that organized, administered, and paid for by the community in which the school was located. In 1900, when young Tireman was just beginning his career as a student, Iowa had a public school system of county independent districts and democratically run township districts though the rest of the nation was centralizing their systems by consolidating rural school districts. Clearly Iowans felt local control was more important than the supposed operational efficiency of consolidated districts. In 1900 there were more than 14,000 schoolhouses in the state and more than 2,500 of them had an average daily attendance of fewer than ten students.³ Literacy statistics attest to the success of the commitment to local control and the paramountcy of the local community in educational matters. The census of 1900 found that Iowa (with Nebraska) had a literacy rate in excess of 97 percent, the highest rate in the nation.⁴

Tireman learned that the classroom was the place where democracy was built, and where citizens learned to take advantage of opportunity. The lesson was well learned. After graduating from Fayette High School in 1913, he attended Upper Iowa State University. Upon graduation in 1917, he proposed marriage to a young woman, Pearl Garretson. The excitement of the imminent wedding ceremony became disappointment when the young man decided that duty demanded he serve in the expanding European conflict.

Characteristically for Tireman duty came first, and so the marriage was postponed.⁵

The two years that elapsed between his graduation from college and return from the war had the effect of directing Tireman onto the course his life was to follow. When he returned from the war he married Pearl and attended a normal school course at Cedar Falls. Soon afterward he became school superintendent at Hanlontown, Iowa. In 1920, he moved to the same position at a larger school in Greeley. From 1922 to 1926, he was the superintendent in Postville.

Iowans valued their schools, but that did not prevent the dour farmers and parsimonious businessmen from expecting full value for the tax dollars spent on education. Schools served as polling places, makeshift churches, and community centers during hours when classes were out. The superintendent was typically the only male among the small faculty and so was expected to be a very versatile educator. Expected contributions to the educational program might include moving furniture, coaching athletic teams, and effectively dealing with recalcitrant and often dishearteningly overgrown students.⁶ Certainly the practical experience, as well as the theories of Progressive education he had read about in textbooks, served to convince Tireman that pragmatism and not tradition was the surer, more humane way to build an educational program.

Experience as administrator and teacher developed in Tireman a flexibility, a readiness to improvise, and a keen awareness of the practical importance of curricular relevance to students. Now and later, he was to follow the dictum that the children were the most important part of schooling. To Tireman schools ought to be, in the fullest sense of that overused term, child-centered. In New Mexico with Hispanic children who could not speak English, he had no trouble developing programs for them since he did not relate to them by means of some theoretical abstraction. They were simply children who needed help.

Somehow, in addition to running schools and organizing teacher institutes, Tireman found the time to continue his schooling. In 1924, during his tenure at Postville, he earned an M.A. degree at the University of Iowa at Iowa City. Pursuing his calling, he went on with his studies in education and psychology at the same institution. In 1927, he quit his job and spent all his time on his studies. The effort was successful; in that year he was awarded a Ph.D. from the University of Iowa.

An anecdote concerning the day he received his final degree and recounted twenty-five years later epitomizes the theme of his life. In 1927, as everything was being prepared for the convocation at which degrees were to be awarded: "Everything was in readiness on the campus. The procession was forming. The band was playing. But a count of the marchers revealed that Loyd was not present. He had been seen down at the railroad yards, so a messenger was sent; he was rushed to the assembly and unshaven and hair askew, a mortarboard was clapped on his head, a gown with purple piping was thrown over his work clothes. On the run he caught the procession and, in turn, was draped with the highly coveted toga, the only man to get a Ph.D. while dressed in a torn work shirt and a pair of levis."[7]

While graduates and well-wishers were involved with the ceremonies, Loyd Tireman had been packing a railroad car with the family furniture and belongings. Typically, he was doing the labor and eager to get on to the next challenge.

Loyd Tireman was a transitional educator, a man whose life and work spanned not only many changes in American life, but embodied many of the ambiguities that confused and harried the nation. Because he placed the needs of students first, he often rose above the characteristic and damaging ethnocentrism of the time. Thus Tireman's personal fairness serves as an example for modern educators.

Many of the transitions and ambiguities experienced in his life arose from history and place. In the Midwest of his childhood and youth, exuberant patriotism sometimes shaded into nativism. Tireman's adult and senior years were spent in the Southwest where frontierlike hardships were paralleled by intense, and sometimes divisive ethnic group loyalties. During his life, war technology moved from trenches and machine guns to jet planes and ballistic missiles. He experienced America's transformation from a land of farmers and dirt roads to one of superhighways and international corporations. He attended one-room schools in which there were not enough textbooks for each student. At his demise there were public schools with sophisticated science laboratories and student bodies of thousands. Schools, in his childhood, were integral parts of local communities. By the mid-twentieth century, when he died, schools had become vehicles in the pursuit of national agendas.

He struggled on a daily basis with the educational implications of social problems that continue to bedevil us today. Growing up in a time and place in which people retreated into prejudice when challenged by social change, he was nevertheless a staunch advocate of cultural sensitivity and was one of the very few to organize bilingual programs. He was trained at the University of Iowa by Professor Ernest Horn, a pioneer researcher and advocate of the use of quantitative methods in the study of educational problems.[8] However, graduate school training did not overcome his innate responsiveness to students, and Tireman was as aware of individual differences and creative needs of students as were Stanwood Cobb, Marietta Johnson, or Margaret Naumberg.[9]

A study of his life reveals that he was one of those historical figures whose direct and tangible contributions have been largely forgotten, though the spirit of his work still exerts great influence wherever educators attempt to create humane and relevant schools. He was an impatient pragmatist, a builder of programs, and an organizer of classrooms. Uncomfortable at his desk, he was happiest striding through an elementary school to see how things were going. His writing demonstrates his personal priorities: it is invariably terse, hurried, verging on fragmentary. Tireman had little time to spend on concern with collegial recognition. He was in too much of a hurry to get on with the work that needed doing.

The high points in Tireman's professional career were three educational experiments in New Mexico in the 1930s: the San José Demonstration and Experimental School; the curriculum revision work generated out of the San José experience; and the Nambé Community School. The foundations of these programs probably evolved from his own early education: community-based education; importance of schooling in forming good citizens; and children's needs forming the core of the school effort.

Perhaps the greatest value of the study of this educator's life and work is the insight it gives those of us living in the troubled present of almost constant educational controversy and adjustments typically labeled reform. The central fact of Tireman's work is the neglect it has received. As a pioneer in bilingual and community education Tireman has been forgotten. A couple of dissertations, a couple of articles, and a rare citation are the only recognitions given him in the contemporary literature.

Historians are supposed to function as the conscious memory of humanity. Educational historians, as chroniclers of that very important, widely involving, and expensive institution, have a heavy responsibility in documenting and recording an inclusive record of our educational past. A clear and comprehensive history of education would communicate knowledge and provide patterns upon which present educators might build and avoid costly errors. Were we all to behave in a rational manner, then history would be complete and would be completely helpful. Alas, we do not function that way.

Scholars, scientists of all types, and especially historians are all too human in being influenced by presentism: the fallacy of using present knowledge to *judge* the past. Presentism leads the unwary to think that since educators in the past were ignorant of modern research methods and sometimes spoke in the ethnically insensitive idiom of their times they have little or nothing to say to us now that is worthwhile. Consequently, outside the pantheon of demigods now accepted as worthy of study, unrecognized past educators are neglected with impunity.

That frame of mind is wasteful and sentences us to the endless cycle of re-inventing wheels that now occupies so much of the time of real and would-be educators. Presentism makes of Dewey, Mann, Rugg, Kilpatrick, and the other stars in educational history something more than fallible humans. Neglect of lesser, though still important, educators is perhaps the most destructive effect of the error of presentism.

The study of Tireman and the experimental programs at San José and Nambé can inform modern education. From his experiences we can learn much about bilingual programs, school community relationships, and the demands of educational reforms.

1
San José Demonstration and Experimental School: The Beginning

The strongly built man with sandy almost reddish hair wearily sat at his desk and tried to compose a letter. He would ask Leo Favrot, his contact at the General Education Board office in Baton Rouge, for some information about his request for funding of a demonstration school. Favrot had always been kind and treated him with understanding, but writing the letter was nevertheless difficult. Loyd Tireman was not a patient man and the waiting had weakened his optimism.[1]

At the beginning of 1930 Tireman had written and submitted to the Rockefeller funded philanthropical organization a plan to organize an experimental school designed to reform education in New Mexico. As he struggled with his letter to Favrot it was spring, and Tireman's frustration was intensified by his certainty that the plan was a good one that would help children. The idea for a demonstration school to serve as a catalyst for educational reform had been taking shape in his mind for almost two years, perhaps longer. His years as a student and then educator in his native Iowa had brought him into contact with some of the strongest reform currents influencing the substance of American public education. But now in New Mexico, when realization of his plan for reform seemed so close, barriers arose to impede the final agreement.

The frustrations must have been particularly galling to Tireman, a man who was used to giving orders and carrying work ahead by his sheer will and energy. He had recently been talking to teachers who had been recommended to him and who would work well in the planned school. Tireman had interviewed a young, enthusiastic educator, Harlan Sininger, and planned to ask him to become principal. Talking with these capable and interested people had kindled his enthusiasm anew, but that emotion only made it harder when he had to tell them they must wait. Soon all teachers would be leaving school and, perhaps, Albuquerque for the summer break, and he would find it difficult to contact them. So much time would be wasted when they could be helping children.[2]

The suspense of the protracted negotiations between the University of New Mexico and the New York City–based General Education Board had worn Tireman down to the point where his request to Favrot for information sounded suspiciously like begging. The energetic professor was unused to asking for favors and was usually far too busy to allow himself to become pessimistic. But the tension of waiting for word from New York, of trying to keep his dream alive, had led him to betray weakness.

Everything now depended on the formal vote of the Board in New York City when they met on May 22, 1930. Tireman asked Favrot to notify him by telegram as soon as a decision was made. The letter reflected Tireman's tension when he wrote: "Each night as I go to bed I am mindful of the approaching 22nd!" Weariness allowed his concern to show when he admitted that "it will be a great disappointment if the plan fails."[3]

Tireman was not disappointed, however. The General Education Board agreed to support the San José School and provided Tireman with a tool with which to develop a curriculum better suited to the educational needs of rural and Hispanic children in New Mexico.

Though Favrot tended to take the tone of an amused and patient older adult speaking to an overeager young man, Tireman's sense of urgency was not hard to understand. Public schools in New Mexico had not been serving Spanish-speaking children in rural areas very effectively and something needed to be done to help them soon. There were few public schools in the poor Hispanic counties in the north, and they were often inadequately equipped and staffed and were open for only a few months of the year.[4]

In 1927, when he was newly arrived in Albuquerque from Iowa, Tireman had quickly immersed himself in the study of the language and reading education of children in his adopted state. He found that very little was known about the performance of the state school system since there had not been an assessment of public school student achievement. At his urging the state agreed to make funds available to conduct a survey of reading achievement in the elementary schools of New Mexico. Tireman was made director of the project, and he drove himself and his assistants so hard that there was a preliminary report ready for the 1928 convention of the New Mexico Education Association.[5]

He reported that "children fail in reading in the beginning grades but very rarely fail in that subject in the upper grades" of the elementary school. In the upper grades, however, there were numerous failures in subjects requiring reading such as history and geography. He concluded that it was a strange development "that a child should pass in reading and fail in the other reading subjects."[6]

Failure in the upper grades, Tireman explained, was probably due to the lack of a purposeful reading program in those years. Children in the primary grades benefited from a clearly structured program, teachers could rely on a detailed reading manual supplied by the state to organize and direct their efforts. The reading manual was "definite and concrete," aiming at clearly defined achievement goals. Emphasis in the upper grades was on subject matter and, though reading well was crucial to student success, there was little planned instruction in reading. As evidence of the confusion, he reported that teachers in the upper grades he talked to were "painfully embarrassed" when asked to list the specific goals of their reading program.

This early report described low reading achievement in the state as a problem that could be alleviated by a revision of the state reading program. Tireman recommended that teachers at all levels of the elementary school make conscious and definite plans for reading instruction. Specifically he urged them to devise exercises "to develop the habits, attitudes and skills essential to economical and efficient silent reading." Competence would be strengthened too were students provided with opportunities in the classroom for recreational reading.

These recommendations would soon be expanded and elaborated. They were the germ of the plan that eventually became the San José Demonstration School. As Tireman traveled about the state continuing the reading survey and speaking to county teachers' conventions, his perception of the problem widened and became more sensitive. When the hundreds of miles of dirt roads had been traversed and the children tested in the tiny, out-of-the-way schools, 9,899 students had been examined. Each of the tests were scored by hand and then various statistical correlations computed. When the enormous output of energy had been made, Tireman had the raw material with which to construct a new curriculum, a curriculum that money from the General Education Board money would allow him to implement.

The findings of the completed survey convinced Tireman that the problems in school achievement in New Mexico included but went far beyond the curriculum. Though the final analysis of the reading survey showed that the reading ability of students in New Mexico did not compare favorably with students in the rest of the United States, that difference was overshadowed by another finding: in New Mexico Spanish-speaking children were farther below the standard than were English-speaking children. Among the youngest children in the survey, those in the third grade, the difference in reading achievement between the two groups was small, but the difference increased in every grade through the eighth.[7] He suggested that a possible interpretation was "the factor of environment." He explained that in the first years of school, when children from both groups were learning to read, "the environment is more nearly equal, since neither English-speaking nor Spanish-speaking children can read at home and much attention is given reading in school." The explicit and strongly focused program of reading instruction in the first three grades mitigated some of the differences in different language environments at home.

After the third grade, however, the differences in home language environment operated more strongly every year. In the higher elementary grades, reading ceased to be a separate subject and became a tool to be used in other subjects. English-speaking students got more practice in reading since their environments were usually richer in opportunities to read in English. Spanish-speaking students did not receive needed help in reading from the school or home.

To help all students, Tireman suggested a reform of the

16 San José

elementary school reading program. To counteract the increasing reading deficits of Spanish-speaking students "a strong reading program must be inaugurated in the intermediate grades." Teachers in those grades should receive special training so that the "excellent work of the first three grades" might go on. The reading difficulties of both groups of students would be alleviated by greater emphasis on silent reading especially in the grades above the fourth. Teachers needed training in the many ways of encouraging silent and recreational reading. Finally, school authorities had to be made to realize the "absolute necessity of adequate libraries."[8]

These recommendations for reform expanded into a plan to organize a demonstration school that might become a catalyst for improvement. As the plan took on a preliminary written form, probably late in 1929 soon after the survey had been completed, Tireman showed the draft to his mentor and friend, Simon Peter Nanninga, dean of the College of Education. Aware of the need for curriculum reform and impressed with Tireman's plan, the dean brought the young professor and his ideas to the attention of President James Fulton Zimmerman.

When President Zimmerman had left Missouri to take up the job of president of the small and struggling state university in 1927, he took on what became a lifetime commitment. Astute and hard-working, totally committed to building the university into a tool for the improvement of the state and region, Zimmerman was an early and successful practitioner of academic grantsmanship.

Nanninga's enterprise in introducing the new faculty member to the new president represented a particularly fortunate coinciding of events. President Zimmerman found Tireman's proposal for the demonstration school provocative and well-planned. In addition, Zimmerman, after several trips to New

York for talks with foundation representatives, had some success in interesting the General Education Board of New York City in the problems of New Mexico.

The General Education Board had been founded in 1902 with enough Rockefeller money to quickly make it a strong influence in education. The original charge to the GEB was that it use its resources to improve Negro education and education generally in the southeastern United States. Zimmerman had successfully convinced the New York officials that New Mexico ought to be considered a southern state and, therefore, a candidate for financial aid.

Having secured that concession from the GEB, Zimmerman was now faced with the problem of submitting a worthy proposal. The need was particularly pressing since plans were being made to entertain the southern agents of the GEB, Jackson Davis and Leo Favrot, on their impending visit to New Mexico. The visit would provide a unique opportunity to impress upon the two agents the urgent needs of New Mexico. What had been lacking was a blueprint for educational reform. Tireman's plan, though rough and preliminary, gave the president the opportunity he needed.

Jackson Davis and his assistant, Leo Favrot, visited New Mexico from January 23 to 25, 1930. In addition to visiting the university and Albuquerque, Zimmerman took the GEB representatives to Santa Fe to meet with the superintendent of public instruction, Atanasio Montoya, and the president of the state board of education, John Milne, who was also the superintendent of the Albuquerque Public Schools. Tireman and Nanninga also sat in on the meetings in Santa Fe. Davis and Favrot were impressed with the people they met and were convinced that rural education in the state needed drastic restructuring.[9]

The GEB report on the trip was probably written by Favrot

and indicates that, while Zimmerman was the chief negotiator, Tireman had done the major portion of the work on the plans for a demonstration school. The report stated that:

President Zimmerman is anxious to take over a Spanish-American school in the vicinity of Albuquerque and operate it with trained teachers as a demonstration school, showing the possibilities of the Spanish-American group, and work out a special adaptations [sic] in the school curriculum as may be found to best meet needs of this group. Dr. Tireman has worked out plans for this project and Dr. Zimmerman would like to undertake it. He thinks he can secure some assistance locally if the Board would aid it.[10]

After a chance to reflect on the information given to them in New Mexico, the GEB representatives reacted to the plans favorably. Jackson Davis wrote President Zimmerman in a manner that must have made the administrator hopeful.

Dr. Tireman's demonstration project appeals very much to Favrot and me. At your convenience can you let us have a statement of your plans and we shall take pleasure in presenting them to the officers of the Board.[11]

Though there were minor editorial changes in the final written version of the plan, the essentials remained the same as when they were conceived by Tireman. The proposed school would perform both training and laboratory functions. As a training site it would help in the preparation of better rural teachers by providing scholarships for those teachers to come to the demonstration school to observe the best teachers using the best methods. Observation and opportunities to use the most modern methods under supervision would equip rural teachers to return to their home schools as more capable and better informed instructors. As a laboratory or experimental school it would collect data on the ability of Spanish-speaking rural students and develop new methods and materials for them. To his dismay, Tireman had discovered that there were no data on these students and much of what went on in schools was based on untested assumptions. He meant for the school to gather information on what Spanish-speaking students could do and subject untested assumptions to careful tests.[12] He had been trained as a researcher, and he was always to seek hard data where others were satisfied with prejudice and conventional knowledge.

While discussions between the GEB and the university continued, Tireman changed some of the wording in response to Favrot's comments. Following advice given him by Favrot, the professor sent the plan for "critical study and comment" to Dr. Kyte, an expert in supervision; Dr. Horn, Tireman's former mentor at the University of Iowa; and Dr. H. T. Manuel of the University of Texas, professor of educational psychology and a recognized expert on the Hispanic population of the Southwest.[13] The three professors evaluated the planned project favorably and their letters of endorsement were forwarded to the New York offices of the Board. Manuel strongly supported the plan. He wrote that he thought Tireman's proposal was an "excellent" one and lent his "enthusiastic approval."[14]

While the written plan for the school met with general support, other crucial negotiations went slowly. In New Mexico there was ready agreement that Tireman's plan was a good one and that the Rockefeller money ought to help. Yet the political interests of the different interested parties required patient negotiations. The basis for cooperation among the university, Bernalillo County, the State Board of Education, and the State Superintendent of Public Instruction had to be worked out. Representatives of the university and the county met to work out agreements whereby the county would turn one of its elementary schools over to the university so that it could become the site of the demonstration school. It is likely that the most delicate negotiations were those involving the university and State Superintendent Montoya. The General Education Board in its educational work in the southeast had established a precedent of working through local state officials. In the January 1930 conversations in Santa Fe the two field representatives had surely made this clear to the New Mexicans. Soon after the trip to New Mexico, Favrot made the board's preference in working through the state officials clear to Superintendent Montoya.[15] The GEB's preferred method of doing business created two related problems for the project. First, since the State Superintendent's office was an elected one, the GEB's precedent placed the proposed demonstration school in the volatile arena of state politics. Second, securing funds locally to support the project was an additional board requirement. It is likely that originally Tireman and Zimmerman expected local funds to come from the state. As the negotiations went on, the financial condition of New Mexico rapidly deteriorated, and a new governor, Arthur Seligman, who was not sympathetic to the university, took office in January 1931. Very quickly the need to generate local funds became a major problem.

The preparation of the formal proposal was hurried along, and in February it was sent off to the board agents. The "Organization" section of the document described the diplomatic arrangements. The Bernalillo County Board of Education agreed to make available "for the use of those cooperating in the experiment" one of its four county schools. In addition the county board promised to grant its regular annual budget to the experimental school for a period of five years. Tireman was to be the director of the school and he was to be advised on policy matters by a board of eight individuals, named as follows: Chairman, Atanasio A. Montoya, State Superintendent of Public Instruction; Dr. James F. Zimmerman, President of the University of New Mexico; Mrs. Edna Rousseau, State Supervisor of Rural Education; Dr. Simon P. Nanninga, Dean of the College of Education, University of New Mexico; Superintendent John Milne, President of the State Board of Education; Dr. B. F. Haught, Head of Psychology Department, University of New Mexico; Miss Marie Balling, Superintendent of Education, Bernalillo County; Dr. Tireman, Head of Elementary Education Department, University of New Mexico.[16]

The proposed membership of the advisory board was one of the two strategic errors made by the authors of the proposal. On the eight-member advisory board there were to be four members representing the university, and six of the eight resided in Albuquerque or its environs. All of the proposed members were educators, only one was Hispanic, and two female. Representatives of business and various interest groups in the local communities were not included.

It is not likely that this imbalance went unnoticed by the representatives of the General Education Board or by local political entities. There is little doubt but that the underrepresentation of spokespeople for rural and Hispanic points of view was quickly brought to the attention of the university. In addition, future elections might bring to office a state superintendent less sympathetic to the proposed demonstration school. This error in the composition of the advisory board was quickly remedied. Membership was expanded to include representatives of groups interested in the project.

In the summer of 1930 the original eight-member advisory board was expanded to seventeen. Added to the board were Senator Cutting and his friend, Mary Hunter Austin, the novelist, feminist, and colonial arts enthusiast. Clyde Tingley, mayor of Albuquerque, and A. L. Krohn, politically active rabbi and president of the Bernalillo County Board of Education, were both invited to join and accepted. Camilo Padilla, editor and advocate of kindergartens, and a group of Anglo and Hispanic businessmen also became members of the board. The expanded group was chaired by Zimmerman, insulating it somewhat from the vagaries of voter affections.[17]

Potentially a far greater strategic error was made in the "Finance" section of the proposal where the funds to run the school were requested. The tentative budget showed a contribution from Bernalillo County of $22,520 a year for five years. The General Education Board was asked to contribute $21,215 for the first year and then $19,500 for the next four years.[18] The document did not indicate any additional funds coming from other local sources.

Leo Favrot promptly responded to Montoya and Zimmerman. Though he complimented everyone involved for a well conceived plan and indicated that he believed that "much good could be accomplished," the communication conveyed a tone of shock that was ominous. As presented, he summarized, the General Education Board was being asked for a commitment of $99,215 over the five-year period. Favrot carefully reminded Zimmerman and Montoya that the earlier conversations had involved a sum of $10,000 a year for five years. They had also been told quite plainly that the "request would be strengthened if you could secure one-half of this amount from other sources. Had the advice been followed the General Education Board's contribution to the project over the five years would have been $25,000."[19]

Favrot went on to convey his surprise at the financial request by telling his correspondents that the request for nearly $100,000 was larger than any they had ever granted for a single undertaking of such a nature.[20] It appeared, he continued, that the County Board of Education was contributing only their annual budget to the running of the school. If that were true and the General Education Board was contributing the total cost of the experimental school, then "it has the appearance of being a project which our Board is promoting" rather than assisting. This violated the policies of the organization. The letter closed with a warning that he did not think the officers of the board would look with favor on the proposal as submitted, assuming he had interpreted the document fairly. Favrot left the next move up to the people in New Mexico with his closing question: "May we not hear from you further about the matter?"[21]

The proposal had upset him so much that Favrot wrote from his Baton Rouge office on the same day to his superior in Richmond, Virginia. To Jackson Davis he repeated his reservations and indicated that he was under the impression that Zimmerman had told them both that he planned to ask U.S. Senator Bronson Cutting for "about half the cost."[22] Davis's reply shared Favrot's concerns, but he wrote that he could find no mention of Cutting in his notes. However, Davis wrote, he fully agreed with his colleague that the New Mexico proposal would be much strengthened were local funds to be raised.[23]

In his prompt reply to Favrot, Zimmerman told him that his interpretation of the proposal had been accurate. The university president presented himself as one who was being pressured from many sides. He indicated that the draft proposal had been submitted to the board in order to be completely honest. Tireman, Zimmerman wrote, firmly believed that financial support of the magnitude indicated in the proposal was necessary. Since the state was suffering the effects of the widening depression and the university from the effects of an unsympathetic governor, President Zimmerman was not op-

24   San José

timistic that he could generate financial support locally. He did promise Favrot that he would take the matter up with some "friends of the university" and would inform him of the progress.[24]

Meetings among concerned parties continued in New Mexico and were duly reported to the representatives of the General Education Board. In the East Favrot and Davis talked the matter over and sought advice from the New York office. They had been impressed by the planned school and by the need for reform in New Mexico. Their commitment to the demonstration school, however, had been shaken by the magnitude of the funds requested. Favrot had been given the major responsibility for carrying on the negotiations and he continued to be cautiously supportive. Using the prerogatives of a diplomatic southern gentleman, after a great deal of thought and discussion, Favrot suggested a tentative compromise to the President of the New Mexico State Board of Education. He knew that John Milne was close to Zimmerman and, by using Milne as an intermediary, he might communicate with the university without committing his organization to anything. In the letter to Milne, Favrot summarized a recent informal discussion he had had with officers of the board. The informal group had arrived at a consensus that they might be able to recommend formally to the full board that a sum of twelve thousand dollars a year for five years be contributed to the proposed school. He explained that the possible GEB support of sixty thousand dollars would still leave almost forty thousand to be raised locally or, failing that, plans for the school would have to be scaled down. Favrot asked Milne to consult with the people involved and let him know of their reactions in time for the next meeting of the board scheduled for May 22, 1930.[25]

When Milne received the compromise offer the pivotal stage

of the negotiations had been reached. Though aware of the need to secure outside funds, Tireman doubtless chafed at the continuing delays. He was sure that children would benefit from the demonstration school. Setting it up and getting on with the reform work was the goal that occupied him. Nevertheless, when Milne presented the Favrot compromise, Tireman joined with Milne and Zimmerman in planning the next step. It seemed to them doubtful that any greater contribution could be expected from the General Education Board, local support offered the only chance to carry out the project on the scale originally planned.

Their efforts began in a promising fashion. They met with Senator Cutting and "were successful in arousing his keen interest." The senator asked Milne, Zimmerman, and Tireman to be patient for a little time before he gave them a definite answer concerning his contribution.[26] Optimism soon became another source of frustration as April passed and the May 22 deadline approached. Senator Cutting went to Washington, D.C. without conveying any message to Zimmerman. Attempts to contact the senator were unsuccessful.[27]

As the days grew warmer Tireman strove to keep up the appearance of high spirits. He could not hope to inspire interest and commitment in the teachers he talked to in April and May if he appeared pessimistic. When he wrote Favrot the second week in May, he let down the facade a little and told the agent how the twenty-second weighed on his mind. The kindly southerner joked with the intense professor a little but promised to wire Tireman as soon as a decision was made "so as to assure you a good night's rest."[28]

All of the planning had not been wasted, however. Soon Zimmerman was able to wire Favrot that Cutting had agreed to give the experimental school five thousand dollars a year for two years and would consider extending the grant if the work proceeded satisfactorily.[29] A week later Davis was able to write Zimmerman that the General Education Board had voted unanimously to contribute twelve thousand dollars a year for five years to the University of New Mexico for the demonstration school which "you and your associates have planned with so much care."[30]

For Tireman the rest promised by Favrot's prompt telegram was likely for only one night. The good news meant a rush to complete the necessary work. After informing Sininger and the teachers selected that the experimental school would be starting up in September, he needed to take the proposal to the people of the San José district. San José had been selected because it was the school and community nearest Albuquerque that was still essentially rural in character. Through the county board, Tireman had met with community leaders and received their reactions to the plans. Assured of the county school board's support and the favorable reception of community leaders, Tireman and Marie Balling, Bernalillo County Superintendent of Schools, met with the people of the San José School district in a mass meeting. "For three hours we explained" and answered questions, he recalled. "At the end of that time they took a vote on the proposition" to support the school. The approval was overwhelming "with only two dissenting voters." He told Favrot that things were moving along satisfactorily but that communication in the near future would be difficult since Tireman was leaving immediately to teach a six-week summer session at the Texas Technological School at Lubbock.[31]

The long and exhausting effort to develop and secure support for a demonstration school that might be used to spearhead reform in rural and Spanish-American education was successfully concluded. Tireman finally had the tool he needed and it was up to him to use it in the best way possible. There was much work to be done.

2

San José Demonstration and Experimental School: The Program

In the fall of 1930, when Tireman returned to Albuquerque from Lubbock, his pleasure in the success of his proposal must have been blunted somewhat by stumbling into a controversy with John Milne. As usual, Tireman was involved in organizing the New Mexico Education Association Conference that was held that year in Albuquerque. He chaired a series of meetings devoted to discussions of rural education problems. After the convention he wrote a short article for the NMEA journal in which he stated he had been "shocked" to learn that the 1930 convention had been the first to offer special sessions on rural education. The article closed with a call for future sessions designed specifically to help rural teachers.[1]

John Milne may well have been the most influential and respected educator in the state. At that time he was certainly the most powerful figure in public education, simultaneously holding the offices of secretary of the NMEA, president of the state school board, and superintendent of the Albuquerque Public schools. In the next issue of the journal Superintendent Milne expressed his sorrow that the young professor had "shocked himself." He went on to remind Tireman that the primary and elementary sections of the NMEA were organized for all teachers who taught in the grades below high school. The elder educator concluded in a didactic tone with a statement that must have received a great deal of agreement from his peers. Milne wrote that "since the same methods and materials are needed to teach both rural and city children perhaps the damage to the rural teachers has not been as great as Dr. Tireman fears."[2]

Throughout its existence San José was faced with no more fundamental obstacles than those habits of thought and normative conventions illustrated in the short, sharp exchange between Tireman and Milne.[3] To the older educator, children, wherever they resided, needed only consistent methods and standardized materials to succeed. Such a view was probably the one held by those who ran the nation's schools. The curriculum was seen as a set of standard requirements to which children were expected to adapt. The obligations of the classroom teacher were to see that the standards were implemented, explained to the students, and progress recorded. Students fulfilled their obligations by working hard to understand that which was presented to them and showing their understanding on tests. In this conservative, assimilationist view of education, schools fulfilled their democratic responsibilities by insuring that what was presented to the students (methods and materials of instruction) was the same for all children no matter what their background. In more general terms, when many of the more traditionalist educators were raising issues in maintenance of standards, or quality, perhaps they were reflecting the nativism and racial prejudice that infected attitudes and behavior in America and the rest of the world between the two world wars.

No other personal trait raises Tireman to a level that demands our attention than that he did not take part in the common nativist and assimilationist sentiments of the time. Despite the popularity of views that held various ethnic groups to be intellectually and, sometimes "morally" inferior, views that were often supported by supposedly scientific evidence, Tireman went his own way. In order to more fully appreciate the strength of the man, his staff, and the uniqueness of the San José program, it will be necessary to understand the context in which the educational experiment occurred.

Among academic researchers the early findings of the differential performances of ethnic groups on intelligence and achievement tests set the tone. An illustration of this kind of assessment apparently based on "hard" evidence, is provided by the book *The Measurement of Intelligence*, authored by the eminent psychologist Lewis Terman. This influential text was probably studied by Tireman in graduate school, and it reported "findings" that were widely accepted. Terman wrote that low average or "border-line" measured intelligence:

> is very, very common among Spanish-Indian and Mexican families of the Southwest and also among negroes. Their dullness seems to be racial, or at least inherent in the family stocks from which they come. . . . Children of this group should be segregated in special classes. . . . They cannot master abstractions, but they can often be made efficient workers. . . . There is no possibility at present of convincing society that they should not be allowed to reproduce, although from a eugenic point of view they constitute a grave problem because of their unusually prolific breeding.[4]

On the national scene among progressive educators who might have been supposed to hold more liberal views on racial matters, there was little attention paid to the particular needs of different ethnic groups. The common tendency among educators was to assume that the proper role of schools was to acculturate minorities so that they might enjoy their role in the American dream. Sessions of the National Education Association during this time also took an assimilationist position.[5]

Two other possible sources of influence on Tireman were his experiences in his home state of Iowa and, later, those he had in Mexico soon after San José opened. In Iowa between the wars, agrarian radicalism and aggressive patriotism had created an environment that was hostile to foreign influences and to anything seen as different.[6] In Mexico, during a quick survey during the summer of 1930, Tireman found that educational policy had vacillated between celebrating local differences and assimilation. There was a broad and strong sense of paternalism among the middle- and upper-class Mexican bureaucrats who administered the rural elementary education programs.[7] Though Tireman was very impressed with many aspects of the Mexican rural experiment, he rejected the racially demeaning implications of some of the policies and statements by Mexican educational leaders.

In addition to opposing widespread prejudice the San José program had to contend with strong local hostility. Both Tireman and the school were targets of attacks by Hispanic politicians and the governor, Arthur Seligman. The politicians, incited by highly publicized racial incidents involving police and courts, sometimes focused on the demonstration school as an example of cultural colonizing.[8] Political opponents of Senator Cutting characterized the school as an Anglo sop tossed to the poor Hispanics. The economy-minded governor, pressed by dwindling taxes resulting from the depression, often forced cutbacks in the university budget. A conservative banker, Seligman tended to see the university and the projects it was involved in as centers of financial mismanagement and waste. As a result, San José sometimes had to curtail special support programs funded through the university or the state department of education.[9]

Despite the many difficulties, the San José demonstration school was organized and soon became an effective force for school reform. That it was able to confound its critics was due to the school's continuing ability to respond sensitively and imaginatively to the needs of the local and state communities.

In 1930, the first year of operation for the San José School, when a typical Hispanic child entered public school in rural New Mexico, he was entering an often incomprehensible and threatening world. Abruptly, at the age of five or six, the child was required to move from the familiar world of the village, a close-knit world of friends, relatives, and the Spanish language, to the unfamiliar one of the classroom. Even were Spanish to be used in the classroom, a not uncommon practice in rural areas when the teacher was a native New Mexican, teaching methods and the impersonality of the classroom made it difficult for him to adapt. By continuing to use Spanish the student was only deferring and intensifying an inevitable clash with the Anglo world.[10] Poor land, weakening prices for farm produce, and the inexorable spread of a money economy made remaining in the village and continuing the practices of one's parents difficult. Quitting the rural, Spanish-speaking life of marginal farming and cattle-raising required participation in an industrial urban setting in which the language of commerce and everyday life was English. Increasingly, economic survival in New Mexico demanded the ability to speak and read English.

Intensifying the problems facing the young Hispanic student in public school was the inappropriateness of the teaching methods in general use in elementary classrooms in New Mexico. Teacher-centered procedures and externally imposed standards of achievement widely used in the East and Midwest and brought to New Mexico by educators trained there had little relevance and less success among Spanish-speaking rural youngsters. Children who had grown up learning by doing were frustrated and defeated by classroom methods that emphasized docility and assumed familiarity with the printed word and abstract principles. The abrupt change from home to school typically resulted in frustration for teachers and failure for the students.

At first for Tireman and his colleagues at the school, the difficulties in successfully teaching reading and, more generally, developing motivation among Hispanic children in school seemed to be a simple problem of method: oral versus silent reading. In New Mexico most elementary teachers still used oral reading procedures. In a classroom using oral reading, one student after another rose and read one or two paragraphs without previous study, and then explained, either in his own words or those of the book, the fragment he had read. In the course of the oral reading lesson, mispronounced words were corrected, inflections and emphases were modified, and some particularly troublesome paragraphs were re-read. After the selection was read, the entire story might be summarized by some of the students.[11]

The oral reading method was best suited to classrooms that were short on resources, a condition that characterized most rural classrooms in the state. If the teacher were not well trained and if there were not enough textbooks for each child to have one, reading aloud from a book was the method of choice. Classrooms in which order and discipline, silence and adult control, were high priorities would also find oral reading suitable.[12]

Though widely used in New Mexico and hallowed through

long use, the oral reading method was considered by Tireman to be inherently counterproductive. The method did not permit all of the students in a class to have extensive practice in reading, practice that was needed if a new language was to be learned. Typically, the text used in recitation detailed incidents and characters that were alien to the students.[13] Since an irrelevant story was told in an unfamiliar language using a method that did not encourage involvement, boredom was likely to be the prevailing attitude in the average New Mexico rural classroom.

In the village of San José, where the experimental school was situated, the public school students showed the long-term results of miseducation common to the rest of rural New Mexico. Students were often held back in grade, so the incidence of "over-ageness" was high. Average daily attendance was low as children regularly avoided the confusing rigors of the classroom and parents saw little point in forcing them to attend. Drop-out rates were high as most students fled school as soon as they could. In general, the San José community had grown used to seeing the public school as a foreign presence that had little relevance to the continuing struggle to make a living.[14]

Added to the educational problems, the village of San José was experiencing a time of rapid economic and social change. Located just south of the Albuquerque city limits with a population of about three thousand, San José was a village quickly becoming a suburb. In 1930 the community and its school of 524 students still illustrated basic patterns of rural existence. Many families had lived in the village for a long time and were related to their neighbors. The community was close-knit and socially stable. Many inhabitants worked small fields located near their homes, or tended small herds of livestock. But things were changing. An increasing number of villagers were going into the city to work as day laborers or domestic help. When the Santa Fe railroad located repair and tie-making shops nearby, the transformation of San José from village to suburb and then neighborhood was accelerated.[15]

The San José Demonstration School became a model for the improvement of rural education in the entire state. Improved methods of teaching Hispanic children were developed and rural teachers came to San José to learn these new methods and use them in their own schools. Tireman and his colleagues recognized quite clearly that the success of any reforms depended on the school's sensitivity to the local community and the involvement of the community in the education of the children.[16] No single unvarying method of instruction would transform student failure into success. Constructive reform depended upon community awareness and the ability of the school to adapt to changing needs.

The pragmatic and responsive nature of the program meant that it was changing and developing all through the seven years that the demonstration school existed. Since the director and principal both encouraged classroom teachers to try out new methods and materials, there were curricular experiments going on all the time. As the school continued, external pressures due to economic depression and budget cuts imposed on the university by Governor Seligman also forced program changes. Successes brought problems as the growing reputation of the San José school led to increased enrollments that strained limited resources. Therefore, the evolving nature of the work of the school means that any general description is somewhat misleading. Nevertheless an attempt to give a sense of the main work of the school and some idea of the innovations it attempted will follow.

The testing program instituted the fall of the first year of the school documented the problems the children were experiencing in achieving the typical age-grade standards. Because of the widespread over-ageness of the students there were likely to be social and self-image problems added to the achievement ones. Therefore, as a policy it was decided that students would not be "reclassified" on the basis of their achievement scores; over-ageness would not be increased. Rather than holding back students who could not do the standard work it was decided to keep children of like age together, except in extreme cases. In the first three grades the teachers divided their students into three ability groups and faculty were assisted in developing different methods and materials for each level. With this decision the San José program aligned itself with the progressive education movement by making the student the central concern and focus. The curriculum reversed the traditional school practice of requiring students to adapt to the subject. At the demonstration school, levels of work typically expected of students in a grade (in other words, the standards) were adjusted to students. Abstract and impersonal standards were no longer imposed as absolute and invariant levels of achievement that every student had to meet. The student was the starting place for the construction of the curriculum.

Working on the assumption that students in the fourth grade and above had had long experience with failure and frustration, the staff developed a more drastic modification of the usual school practice. Students in these grades who tested below their San José peers in general aptitude and reading achievement were moved to an "Opportunity Room." There the students received individualized instruction and greater individual attention than in the regular classroom. The aim of the "Opportunity Room" was to bring the skills of the youngster up to the level of his peers so that he might return to his regular classroom. There was a great deal of emphasis on drill in skills, peer tutoring, and the use of community resources in this room.

Another program innovation involved the work done in the pre-first classes. The pre-first grade antedated the San José school and had evolved as a method of helping children who came to school knowing little or no English. When they started school English-speaking children would begin the regular work of the first grade. Spanish-speaking children coming to school at the same age would spend their first year in a pre-first class learning English. Over time the original purpose of the pre-first class became diffused and the work of the first year for Hispanic children tended to become a watered down, remedial, version of the first grade.

While recognizing the social and emotional problems often created for these students by holding them back a year behind their English-speaking peers, Tireman recognized the pre-first class as a permanent part of the system and attempted to make the pre-first work at San José as effective as possible. In the pre-first classes at the school the work concentrated on the acquisition of English and building a vocabulary. Holding Hispanic students back a year relative to their Anglo peers could only be justified if the retention resulted in the future school success of the Hispanic students.

After the experiences of the first year of operation of the experimental school, Tireman and Sininger contemplated organizing a "junior pre-first" class. In the proposed class, Spanish-speaking children would come to school at the age of five and be given a year of English language instruction and enrichment. After the preschool experience these children would be able to enter first grade at the same age as their Anglo schoolmates and, it was hoped, compete with them on equal terms. Unfortunately Tireman never got the chance to try out this promising program.

Instruction at San José was based on "an activity program."[17] This program was based on two principles that seemed to Tireman and the school staff to be especially valuable in dealing with the Spanish-speaking children. First, the activity program created more interest among students because actually doing something was more engrossing than "reading how someone else does it." Second, active participation in doing or making something led to better understanding and longer lasting learning than an abstract presentation in a book did.

The activity method did not reject learning from books but sought to develop a better balance between passive reading and active exploration. Children would learn more rapidly and keep the ideas longer if reading about a principle was interspersed with opportunities to work with tangible examples of it. A textbook discussion of conservation of soil meant more when students could see the effects of rain washing topsoil into irrigation ditches, when they could compare a well-kept field with one that had been overgrazed.

Earlier Tireman outlined the goals of a reading program when he wrote that reading was not a close relative of declamation but was thinking through the use of the printed page. Learning how to read was learning how to think. To be successful, reading had to become a tool that was used eagerly by youngsters, a problem-solving tool. He said that for reading to become an effective tool "thought-getting" from the printed page must become "commonplace." Students must be helped to see reading as a source of useful ideas, not an exotic exercise performed to gain adult approval.[18]

The San José School used recreational reading and student interest to enrich and expand the reading curriculum. When the demonstration school began, books were purchased for recreational reading and class use as fast as the students could use them. Times were set aside every day so that students might pick out books and read them in the classroom. Every classroom had a small library of books, and students were allowed to take them home for short periods of time. Teachers visited the homes of their children to encourage parents to support the work of the school and read to the students.

Both reading and general schoolwork paid little attention to conventional grade-level standards, each grade began with whatever books the students could read most readily. "The third grades read all the primers and second grade books they needed" before they took up third grade readers. In the sixth, seventh, and eighth grades formal textbook work was supplemented with readings from the daily newspapers. These articles allowed the children to practice reading English as it was used in practical ways. Reading newspaper articles also provided an opportunity to discuss current events, local government, state politics, and other important local issues.[19]

The philosophy undergirding the methods used to promote English language acquisition experiences were illustrated most clearly when teachers took their students out for a walk. Fourth graders, students of any age, undoubtedly enjoyed the chance to stretch their legs and get out of stuffy classrooms on warm days. Pictures of the school from the 1930s show that it was shaded by some trees and there were a few dwellings near it. Most of the land around the school building was open and was used as pasture, plowed fields, or gardens.[20]

The walks the children and their teachers took provided opportunity for concrete illustrations of what they had discussed in the classroom. Birds and animals, cultivated crops and trees, might revive a previous discussion about science and botany. Students might be inspired to talk about how their parents and relatives farmed or cared for their herd. Gardens might introduce opportunities for discussions about nutrition and hygiene. All of these observations provided occasions for language usage, essential practice in vocabulary and pronunciation.

The students took the benefits of the walk back to the classroom and used them as foundations upon which to build. In the classroom the teachers typically used a language experience approach to strengthen students' reading skills. In the San José approach to reading individual children were encouraged to talk to the teacher about the walk and what they learned. The teacher helped the student to orally compose a short story detailing whatever it was that had most interested him on the walk.

From the conversations with individual students the teacher developed two types of learning aids for future lessons. She compiled a list of words from student observations for future vocabulary practice. The short story the child composed was printed by the teacher on a poster board. After drawing a scene to illustrate the story and decorating the poster, the child used his own story to study English.[21]

The instructional program not only built on the intrinsic motivation derived from having the child learn language from his own compositions, but also capitalized on the interest children had in their native language. A unique part of the San José curriculum was the inclusion of formal instruction in the Spanish language.

The existence of the bilingual program at San José ran counter to several powerful trends in American society and public education. Influenced by the post–World War I wave of nativism, educators in the United States, teachers as well as theorists, tended to view home language as something that had to be changed. Whether it was English as used on the streets or a European language of immigrant parents, school usually saw its collective function as bringing the language of students up to the traditional standards of English usage in speech and writing. Therefore, though there were some notable exceptions, in the typical public schools of the time there was little concern with bilingual education. Though progressive education's general desire to put the child and his background at the top of the priority list would eventually provide the opening for bilingual education to enter the curriculum, in the 1930s most educators still believed that providing standardized educational experiences for all children would result in social equality.

It seems that Tireman first became interested in bilingual education as a result of his trip to Mexico in August 1930. He traveled in Mexico to observe rural elementary schools and to collect ideas that might work at San José. Though the Mexican schools he saw did not have bilingual programs, they strongly emphasized a curriculum suited to the background of their students. The Mexican emphasis on relevancy impressed him, and it seems that bilingual education for Spanish-speaking children in New Mexico was a logical result. What began on a small scale at San José soon became a successful effort that played an increasing role in the total program.[22]

At the winter meeting of the San José School Board of Directors in 1931, the first meeting after his return from Mexico, Tireman recommended that a teacher be employed to teach Spanish.[23] The program the director had in mind was a modest one involving all of the children in grades one through eight. In the first five grades, all students would receive one thirty-minute period of instruction a day. For sixth, seventh, and eighth graders Spanish instruction was to be elective.[24] Despite the fact that professional judgment supported the new program, the proposal resulted in a long discussion. Financially it did not seem to be a propitious time to add to the curriculum. The depression had eroded state and local sources of support and the economic pressures on the demonstration school did not seem likely to ease. Just when economic pressures were increasing, the success of the school had led to increased expenditures. Average daily attendance, a statistic that could be an index of popularity and relevance of the school program among parents, had increased over the first year and the rise would continue. As more children attended school more regularly, overhead costs, as well as expenditures for books and materials rose. Despite these concerns Tireman's arguments carried the day and a teacher of Spanish was hired for 1932.

After a year of the bilingual program Favrot, during his regular inspection, observed that the training in Spanish seemed to help all of the students. He found that the instruction seemed to be especially good for the minority group of Anglo children in the school.[25] Language development of English-speaking children was not interfered with by learning a second language. These students also showed a more tolerant attitude toward students from Spanish backgrounds.

Favrot reported that the director and staff felt that the bilingual program awakened in Hispanic students an appreciation of their linguistic and literary heritage. Spanish classes also provided an additional way to improve students' comprehension.[26] Bilingual classes provided Spanish students an opportunity to compete on an equal footing with their English-speaking peers. Parents and other community people saw the positive effects of the language classes on their children and so were further impressed by the sensitivity and responsiveness of the school.[27]

The problems of language and education continued to fascinate and challenge Tireman. In the United States there was relatively little attention being paid to bilingual education, and so his attention turned to Europe. Early in 1933 he proposed to the General Education Board that he be granted a fellowship to spend a year in Europe observing various national bilingual programs.[28]

His decision was made despite the problems involved. While the university would grant him leave for a year there was no chance at all of the institution giving him any financial support. The depression had recently forced the university to cut its budget by 25 percent.[29] Therefore, the planned European trip could be realized only were he to secure outside support. Fortunately, the New York–based foundation decided to support Tireman's sabbatical plan and awarded him thirty-five hundred dollars.[30]

He first visited England to observe a teacher training college that specialized in preparing teachers for bilingual classrooms. From there he went to Wales to observe bilingual methods used in elementary classrooms. By the end of October, he had seen much though he wrote Favrot that he was disappointed that the English and Welsh had no data to support their claims. Everything, he found, was decided as a result of the "concensus of opinion."[31]

In Europe he visited schools in Switzerland and France where he found that classroom methods were quite formal and teacher-centered. When he explained to European educators what was being done at San José and sought advice, he received what he considered facile and unsatisfactory responses: do what we do, use the European model. In general terms the European model was to use the children's "mother language" as the language of instruction for the first few years of school and then introduce the language of the majority. Perhaps that would work, he wrote his friend, in countries where the mother language was widely used and was supported by an articulate nationalist sentiment. That did not seem to describe the situation in New Mexico, and so a transplanted European system of bilingual education might not work well at all. While Tireman's pedagogical conclusions may have been accurate, the implication that there was little political organization or ethnic sentiment among Hispanics showed an ignorance or blindness that was to interfere with his work in the future. In this respect, the reformer showed the influence of his times and exhibited a kind of cultural missionary attitude.

Ultimately the trip that began so eagerly and hopefully ended in disappointment. The director of the San José school did not believe he had received the useful ideas he had hoped for from European educators, and the unfavorable exchange rates for the U.S. dollar meant that his money was soon gone. By the end of January 1934 Tireman was forced to return to New York.[32]

After visiting some eastern progressive schools Tireman returned to Albuquerque. At the next meeting of the San José School Board of Directors he reported his judgment that European bilingual education methods were not superior to those being used at the school. In partial support of his assertion he was able to cite the results of some testing that had been done. During the previous year "using an accepted high school, first year, Spanish test" sixth graders at San José had been assessed. They had a median score of 45.5 while the test norm was 40. On a second year Spanish test, San José seventh and eighth graders had a median score of 91 and the norm was 70.33. The best news of all, the director reported, was that "the children have acquired the ability to read and write Spanish with any appreciable" interference with their ability to do the same in English.[33]

The report of the first four years of the San José school effort put the problem of language and school into a wider setting. The document indicated that throughout New Mexico 10 to 15 percent of the Spanish-speaking students left school before the third grade. The unresponsive schooling that these youngsters received was a "contributory factor in this tremendous loss."[34] It seemed a great shame to Tireman and the other authors of the report that children who have a natural advantage in speaking Spanish should be deprived of the advantage "until they get into high school, there to study Spanish as a foreign tongue." The San José school had developed a unique bilingual program that offered Spanish instruction to elementary school children. Tireman and his colleagues urged that the bilingual program developed at San José be considered as a partial solution to the educational problems of Hispanic children in the state and region.

At the summer meeting of the Board of Directors in 1934 it was reported that while enrollment for 1933–34 was practically the same as for 1930–31, the average daily attendance had increased by fifty-nine. Students were attending with greater regularity, documenting that school efforts to make the curriculum more relevant and to involve the community had been successful.

The demonstration school treated the goal of community involvement from the beginning as something more important than occasional parent nights. When Tireman had visited Mexican rural elementary schools as San José was starting up, he had been very favorably impressed with the efforts of these schools to improve relations with the village community. In Mexico alongside traditional schoolwork there were efforts to teach the students better hygiene and ways to deal with the immediate problems of food and survival. There had been annexes attached to the Mexican schools where students might raise rabbits or learn handicrafts, applying in practical ways the things they learned in the classroom.[35]

Though the situations in rural Mexico and San José were not the same, educationally the New Mexico setting presented a similar challenge. The San José community had grown used to seeing public school as something apart, something foreign. This view had been reinforced by the separation of the school from the life of the community.

The problem of education in the rural villages of New Mexico is more than the problem encompassed by the four walls of the school room; it is to bring the community and the school into harmony, to vitalize the school curriculum by inclusion of life situations, to remove the school from a sequestered and isolated position and to make it the center of interest and effort of all. . . .[36]

In Mexico Tireman had noted that a prominent feature of the classrooms was sessions devoted to instruction in personal health and hygiene.[37] The importance of the children's health was a matter upon which educators and community could easily agree. One of the first acts of the staff at the demonstration school was to set up a health screening program. The eyesight of each child was checked and a special fund, the result of private donations and a benefit show put on by students and staff, was raised to buy glasses for those in need.

The county school nurse was brought in to examine all of the children at the school, and two hundred and forty-nine were found to be in need of some kind of attention. Teachers and the nurse visited homes in order to persuade parents to have their children treated. The suspicion and unease of the parents toward the alien practices of medicine were partially allayed by the program of home visits.[38]

Among the most successful efforts of the school to reach out into the village and enlist adults in the work of the school was the program of Spanish Colonial Arts and Crafts. Under the direction of the talented and energetic Mela Sedillo, with the financial support of the vocational office of the state government, a one-room annex to the main school building was built employing community and student labor. Once the building was erected, the boys immediately set to work learning woodwork by building furniture for the annex.[39]

The first year every child was given a chance to experiment with each of the crafts of woodworking, tin, and leather crafting, as well as preparing and weaving wool. Thus all of the children gained firsthand knowledge of their artistic heritage. In this way it was also hoped that each child might find some craft at which he was talented. Soon some of the best of the young workers were able to sell some of their products. Parents and community artisans were shown in a practical manner that the school was involved in the life of the community.[40]

The program at the San José Demonstration school had an immediate and beneficial impact on the children and the community. For the state of New Mexico, though, the paramount concern was the effectiveness of the experiment in changing classrooms throughout the rest of the state. Indeed, it is likely that the major selling point that convinced the General Education Board to support the effort was the goal of influencing rural education throughout the state. The San José teacher training program and the later program to revise public school curriculum were the two main vehicles used to effect progressive reforms. These programs are discussed in the next chapter.

3
San José and New Mexico: Teacher Training and Curriculum Revision

Tireman was inexhaustible in traveling about the state and region to spread the message. Education, he urged again and again, must change in fundamental ways. Public schools had to learn to become more responsive to their students. Schools had to become community resources relevant to the needs of the local community. In letters to Favrot the professor stated that he recognized that schools changed slowly. He realized that peoples' values and ideas changed slowly. But intellectual recognition did not mean that Tireman ever learned to emotionally accept institutional inertia. Tireman could never be satisfied with gradual or partial reform.

To him it was crystal clear that the whole fabric of public education in New Mexico required change. If old habits, if inertia, if racial prejudice supported by the new and growing testing movement, interfered, then Tireman would seek to effect change by the strength of his arguments and his will power.[1]

His goals for reforms were made clear in many speeches but never so clearly as in one he gave in the early days of the San

José experiment. Addressing a convention of rural educators in Colorado, he detailed his experiences in Mexico, placing emphasis on the efforts of Mexican elementary educators to discover and meet the needs of the villages. He described how, before setting up the demonstration school, efforts had been made to involve the San José community. Curriculum had been developed to include parents in the education of their children. After citing examples of reforms tried out at San José, Tireman directed a series of questions to those listening. These questions constitute the goals of the San José school and foreshadow later efforts at Nambé.

teachers will tend to reproduce in their schools what they learned in the classrooms of the colleges. Is it too much to ask those who prepare rural teachers for the Spanish-speaking people if they are really doing so? Do our Spanish-speaking people need fractions, decimals, grammar? . . . Or do they need teachers who will show them how to plant proper vegetables, how to achieve more economic freedom, how to feed their children properly, how to improve community relations?

The address ended with a call to his colleagues urging them to rise to the opportunity. "We have a rare opportunity to be educational pioneers."[2]

The clear impact of the speech was that institutions of higher education in New Mexico and the Southwest were not doing a very good job preparing teachers who would teach rural Hispanic children effectively. To correct that failure would require professors of education to recognize the problems and then train teachers to remedy those educational problems. At San José Tireman aimed to deal with the reform of teacher education in several ways.

Yet the speech, as eager as it was to recruit teacher educators to the reform movement, implied that the aim of education relevant to Hispanics was to keep them in the village. It could be read that Tireman was advocating an education that would produce happy and satisfied villagers. To Hispanics energetically involved in forcing their way into college and marketplace, such sentiments as those voiced by Tireman were dangerous ambivalences at best. At the worst, he was lining up with those who were involved in limiting opportunities for Hispanics. In later writings he was to clarify his position and make it quite clear that a good and relevant education opened up opportunities. By that time it was too late.

A major effort at the demonstration school was focused on training new and retraining experienced classroom teachers. As the work at the demonstration school continued, the teacher preparation component was expanded into a program that not only offered instruction but also involved an energetic scheme of following up and supporting the teacher when she returned to her district. This support program was eventually taken over by the state education department and became the basis of state supervision and assessment efforts. What was learned at San José also led to a statewide effort to evaluate and reform the public school curriculum.

The teacher training program depended on local district support and initiative. County superintendents submitted names of teachers from their areas who might profit from a period of study at San José. Tireman, Sininger, and a subcommittee of the Advisory Board picked the individual teachers who were invited to attend a three-month training session in the fall or spring term. The only requirements for the award were that the teacher work in a rural area and teach primarily Spanish-speaking children. In the first year of operation, before the school was well-known, it was required that applicants also have a high school diploma and hold a teaching job.[3]

At first, some of the teachers who attended San José were poorly prepared, and so the training they received was concentrated on the teachers' own reading and writing skills. As the reputation and purpose of the school became more widely known, the quality of the cadet teachers (as the teacher-trainees were later termed at San José) improved, and more of their time at the training school could be devoted to advanced training in bilingual skills and problems of rural education.

There was also a shortage of trained principals for small rural schools in the state. The College of Education had created from its own funds five, five-hundred dollar scholarships to combat the shortage. These scholarships were to go to mature and experienced teachers who would return to college to take classes and work at the demonstration school as well. Though it was expected that the scholarship holder would finish a course of studies resulting in a degree within one academic year, financial support might be renewed. When their studies were finished, graduates would return to their home districts and take up jobs as principals of small rural schools.[4] Individual and institutional financial problems caused this program to have a very uneven history.

Cadet teachers were expected to put in long days at San José as they assisted regular teachers, observed in their classrooms, and attended regular lectures by school and college faculty. A typical day for a cadet teacher began at 8:00 A.M., an hour before the students arrived. The cadet and regular teacher would discuss the work of the day to come and get the room ready for the children. As the children began arriving, the cadet was expected to be out on the playground to organize games and generally supervise. The school day went by in what must have been an exhausting flurry of observations and cadet-prepared lessons as well as the normal demands of twenty-five or thirty youngsters. Cadets observed and taught lessons in every subject in the elementary school curriculum.

When the children went home at 3:45, no doubt ready for a snack and a rest, cadet teachers had a few minutes respite before they had to attend their own class. From four to five every day Tireman taught a class in methods of elementary education in rural schools and used the class to discuss the insights into students and education that had been gained at San José. Later the cadet teachers might discuss their own observations and experiences. In the evenings the cadets were expected to study, prepare posters for the next day, and take part in the planned social program. The evening program, more likely than not, involved a lecture or a visit to an exhibit or museum. On Saturdays the cadets were given a half-day off. Before they were able to relax though, they attended classes in music, crafts, and games. A lecture by Tireman or one of his colleagues from the college was usually on the schedule.[5]

As the teacher training program developed, two problems plagued the staff. One problem was the disparity the staff felt existed between the "ideal" setting of San José and the real school and community environment to which the cadets would return. Inexperienced teachers needed to observe improved classroom teaching methods and materials in a setting that approximated their own home school. In this way they might see more clearly the appropriateness and effectiveness of the things being taught at San José.

The second problem was one of continuing support for the cadet once she returned to her home school. Once away from the supportive atmosphere of the demonstration school, habit and collegial pressure would probably prove stronger than the techniques learned at San José. Also, on a more positive side, the trained cadet brought back with her to her home school many tools and insights that needed to be demonstrated and explained to her colleagues. No mechanism to address these problems of dissemination and adequate supervision yet existed in the state.

The problem of disparity was dealt with first at San José. After the first year the Opportunity Room (that had taken students in the fifth through eighth grades with deficits in basic skills) was expanded to include students from all grades. In addition, a trained rural demonstration teacher from the University of Michigan was hired to manage the Opportunity Room.[6]

This arrangement was not satisfactory since it burdened the Opportunity Room with two jobs, one remedial and the other demonstration, that were sometimes not compatible. In 1932 the demonstration problem was solved when an agreement was reached with Bernalillo County and the village of Cedro in the mountains east of Albuquerque. There, about twenty miles from the city, the university, through its program at San José, assumed control of the one-room school at Cedro. A house for a resident teacher was built and a member of the San José staff became the resident teacher. Cadet teachers regularly visited the demonstration one-room school at Cedro to see exemplified in practice, in a real rural school setting, methods and materials they were told about at San José.

The program at Cedro was fortunate in selecting Jennie Gonzales as the first teacher. She was a hard worker, an effective teacher, and an able advocate. At the 1932 New Mexico Education Association convention Mrs. Gonzales gave a speech describing what the program was trying to accomplish in the village. She also gave several demonstration lessons illustrating methods employed at the one-room school.[7] Later she left Cedro to become the rural school supervisor for the state. In 1933 Rose Prieto, Mrs. Gonzales's successor at Cedro, gave a series of very popular demonstrations for the state educational association convention.[8]

The Cedro demonstrations were supplemented by the annual open house days scheduled at the San José Demonstration school. All of these sessions helped publicize the university-sponsored work in rural education and may have encouraged more able and committed teachers to apply to the program. The convention demonstrations and open house sessions also provided practical illustrations of some of the curriculum principles and practices that were being developed at San José. Rural teachers who attended the sessions perhaps carried away with them a little curiosity concerning the activity method and the language experience approach of teaching reading. Slowly the stage was being prepared for wider reforms.

While offering training to twenty-four rural teachers a year constituted a great step ahead in improving the education of Hispanic children, Tireman and the San José staff were painfully aware that their efforts did not solve the educational problems of the state. To spread more widely the specific activities and applications of methods being developed at San José, the director and staff developed a series of mimeographed bulletins to be mailed out to 540 rural teachers in the state. These bulletins offered general information on such topics as: Seat Work, the Bulletin Board, and Methods of Presenting New Words. Some of the newsletters described things to do: A Zoo Activity, A Cotton Project, and Japan and the Silk Industry.[9]

The problem of supervision, insuring that what was learned at San José was applied locally, was dealt with by the evolving plan of Key Schools within a County Extension Program. Certain schools centrally located in a rural region of a county were identified as Key Schools. Initially teachers who had finished their training at San José would meet at the Key

Schools to share their ideas and materials with their colleagues. Later San José assumed a more active role when in July 1932 the State Board of Education agreed to support a County Extension field worker to expand the Key School plan. Marie Hughes, who was to have a long and distinguished career in early childhood education, was hired to fill the job of field worker. She immediately undertook her work with great energy and imagination.

Between September 17, 1932 and April 5, 1933 the field worker spent 115 days in the field traveling over ten thousand miles visiting 111 teachers in seventy-eight schools. In addition, in this period she organized sixteen all-day demonstrations for a total attendance of 400 people.[10]

Whether her work was with two teachers in a secluded rural school or several teachers in a larger school, the field worker's plan of instruction was much the same. The sessions typically ran from nine in the morning to four in the afternoon, and began with Mrs. Hughes giving a demonstration lesson illustrating the recommended way of organizing and teaching the subject. Because of its importance, reading was often the subject for the demonstration lesson. After the demonstration lesson, Mrs. Hughes explained to the teachers what she had done in order to focus attention on particularly important features. The teachers might ask her questions and inspect any of the materials she had used. The final portion of the day would be spent with the teachers practicing the methods they had observed and making materials for future use.[11] To supplement the training sessions several packets of materials made up of suggested reading activities, seatwork, vocabulary, and a description of a circulating library of professional books was sent to the cadets.[12]

The effectiveness of the county extension program in publicizing the San José training program as well as improving the quality of instruction in rural areas was clear. The seven counties originally served by the extension program were soon joined by others eager for the training. The success of the work encouraged the state to provide state supervisors for rural education. As the state took over the work of the County Extension Program the San José school discontinued this work in May 1934. Marie Hughes remained at the San José School and later replaced Harlan Sininger as principal when he left to become director of teacher training at Highlands University.[13]

In 1935 the original funding of the San José Demonstration school by the General Education Board was nearing completion. When Tireman, Nanninga, and Zimmerman decided to seek renewed support from the New York foundation the proposal was not met with immediate approval by the GEB. Despite the successful work, the project's future was not assured.

Doubts concerning future support did not arise from any reservations about the quality of the work being done at the school. Leo Favrot consistently gave laudatory annual evaluations of the reform efforts in New Mexico. There was a slight tendency for the sophisticated professionals in the New York office to privately assess Tireman and his colleagues as overeager territorials. However, this attitude was balanced by a recognition of the importance of the work being done in New Mexico and the skill with which the program was administered.

If the executives of the GEB were ever inclined to minimize or dismiss Favrot's assessments, there were examples of favorable inspections of the San José school by officials not officially connected with the GEB. President Tormey of the Arizona State Teachers' College at Flagstaff had visited the school and been very impressed. His enthusiasm for the San José program led him to invite Tireman to Arizona to assist in setting up a similar demonstration and experimental school affiliated with the Arizona institution.[14]

When the president of the Julius Rosenwald Fund of Chicago, Edwin R. Embree, took a working vacation in the west, he included a visit to the demonstration school near Albuquerque on his agenda. His organization had ties of friendship and shared mission with the GEB, so he might have been inspecting the school as a favor for his friends in New York. Upon his return to Chicago, he promptly penned a highly complimentary letter to his friend, the president of the GEB, Trevor Arnett. Rhetorically he asked Arnett how his organization consistently "searched out and supported" remote and deserving projects. Of the school he said:

Particularly we were impressed by the work which Professor Tireman has done at the San José school and by the influence which this experiment has carried widely through the state. . . .[15]

Early in 1935 the university submitted a formal request to continue San José for three years with reduced financial support. During this extension Tireman stated in the proposal that he wanted to further investigate the language abilities of Hispanic children and develop an exemplary reading program for them.[16]

Probably a major reason for the hesitant response of the GEB to the university's plans was that the New York organization was going through a difficult period of reassessment and reorganization. Board resources had been seriously depleted by the depression and by a policy that allowed extensive grants from capital funds. This had led to a growing feeling that the board was overcommitted.[17] As a result executives with somewhat conservative views were taking over control of the benevolent foundation and reviewing its direction.[18]

The fate of the requested funding extension was dealt another blow by the sudden death in 1935 of Senator Cutting in an airplane crash. Earlier he had given assurances to Zimmerman and Tireman that his financial support for San José would continue for three years. Since the senator's money constituted the major source of local support required by the GEB, the setback was a major one. After the senator's death, the promised funds were contingent on the extremely delicate task of securing his widow's approval and the glacial movement of the probate court.

Through the spring, Zimmerman pressed the trustees of the Cutting estate for a decision while he assured the GEB of the commitment of the university to the San José project.[19] Such statements of institutional commitment by Zimmerman were probably little more than brave words of moral support since the university continued to experience severe financial problems. Favrot quite likely continued his quiet, strong support for the New Mexico reforms among his GEB colleagues. The school director and his staff worked intensively on a report describing the programs and improvements effected at San José.

Tireman's report and the GEB's approval of the three-year extension, at a reduced level, crossed in the mail. Once again a tense and difficult waiting time, punctuated by crises, had ended favorably for the university. The experiment at San José would survive for three more years.

Never a man to rest on his laurels or to be satisfied with just continuing a program, Tireman eagerly surveyed the next problem. With the short-term future of the demonstration school assured, he turned his attention to the education of all rural children in the state. He was impatient to use the experience gained at San José to reform education throughout New Mexico. Used effectively, what had been learned at the school could also make the training of school teachers more relevant to student needs and force older faculty in public schools out of their ruts.

The plan that Tireman developed grew out of his familiarity with GEB support of state curriculum-revision projects in the southeastern United States. He developed a plan and sent it to New York that proposed a statewide program of curriculum study and revision for New Mexico. With the demonstration school funded for three more years, an effective point was made that curriculum reform in New Mexico was a logical extension of the work being done at San José. The clear implication was that for the GEB to do otherwise would be to waste much of the work and money expended at the demonstration school.[20]

While the state curriculum-revision plans were being reviewed in New York, Tireman and Zimmerman carefully built support in New Mexico. They explained the curriculum study plans to the NMEA leadership, members of the state board of education, and the presidents of the other teacher-training institutions in the state. The proposal was revised to conform to suggestions made by other educators and their organizations. The proposed curriculum revision received a big boost when Tireman and Zimmerman gained the strong support of H. R. Rodgers, state superintendent of public education.

Rodgers was such an enthusiastic supporter of the planned program of curriculum reform that he traveled to Leo Favrot's office in Richmond, Virginia, to inform Favrot of the state's support of the project.[21] One month later the New Mexico state superintendent of public education met with Favrot in St. Louis to again urge the foundation's support for the reform plans.[22]

Favrot's advocacy and the careful in-state recruitment of support for the New Mexico curriculum plans apparently outweighed GEB worries about resources. Superintendent Rodgers was informed on April 27, 1936 that the GEB had agreed to fund the program to revise curriculum for rural schools in the state. The GEB agreed to make available six thousand dollars a year for three years. The state and the university agreed to provide additional support to the project. Subtle urging by the funding organization resulted in Tireman being appointed director of what was initially called the New Mexico Program of Curriculum Revision.

At Tireman's urging the program was soon renamed the Program for the Improvement of Instruction to emphasize that the focus of the effort was on the classroom and the goal of improving the relationship between student and teacher. In Tireman's words, the aim of the program was "the improvement of the whole environment" of the school. The first step in the Program for the Improvement of Instruction had been taken earlier by the State Board of Education when it raised the certification requirements for teachers.[23]

The next step was to develop teacher involvement in the program. It was essential to make them aware of the state reform program and provide opportunities for them to respond to common educational problems. Unless teachers were made to feel that they had an important role and that their suggestions were valued, the curricular reform efforts were not likely to be successful.

To encourage cooperation and involvement the program divided the state into districts with a local educator in charge as assistant director. Assistant directors worked with county officials to develop a county plan, form committees, and invite teachers to join the committees. Efforts in the districts and counties were aided by a study booklet prepared by Tireman and the San José staff. The booklet contained suggested discussion topics and ways in which to analyze and assess classroom instruction and school management.

Every committee was encouraged to set its own goals and agendas. Curriculum materials developed around the state by the committees, or by enterprising individuals, were sent to the curriculum laboratory at the University of New Mexico. The laboratory was managed by Marie Hughes, who had been associated with the San José school for several years and who was assisted by Laura Atkinson.

The suggestions, exercises, and other curriculum materials that arrived from the districts were reviewed and, perhaps, revised at the laboratory. The most promising materials were then tried out in volunteer test schools in Valencia and Torrance counties. Mary Watson, a former rural teacher, was the field worker in charge of the testing of materials at the schools.[24]

Most school districts were actively involved in the program to improve instruction. County involvement took many forms. In some areas school drop-out rates were computed and student motives for leaving school were surveyed. Library resources were organized, catalogued, and compared to what was needed for adequate support of the instructional program. Teachers in Doña Ana County prepared a questionnaire and canvassed homes in order to carry out an assessment of illiteracy.[25] Such local projects produced information on many educational problems that had never existed before. As data became available on the problems, teachers had an opportunity to suggest solutions and take part in implementing them.

The curriculum laboratory played a passive but critical coordinating and disseminating function in the reform work. Sample curricula, study guide reports, and suggested classroom activities were sorted and filed at the laboratory. Teachers and administrators were invited to use the files when they were in

Albuquerque. Teacher requests for copies of reports and general advice were also responded to by the staff.

The university facility also served a more active, initiating role in the reform of instruction. Both Tireman and Hughes put the lessons learned at San José as well as the insights gathered from experience into a series of booklets designed for the classroom teacher. Aided by Laura Atkinson, a young education student and illustrator, these materials to help teachers were an expansion of the short bulletins sent out earlier by the demonstration school. The lonely and often undertrained rural schoolteacher in New Mexico was at last receiving support and an opportunity to improve her contribution to the education of young children.[26]

Early in 1936, at his Richmond, Virginia, offices, Favrot received a carefully worded and no doubt surprising letter from Tireman. The communication informed him that the Program for the Improvement of Instruction was "going on nicely." Continuing, the letter indicated a need to confer with the GEB representative soon. Despite the urgency, Tireman wrote, "the matter should be presented to you personally" rather than conveyed in a letter. The matter that needed to be discussed had to do with the San José school, and it was suggested that they meet at the NEA convention in New Orleans in February.[27]

Tireman and Nanninga, the dean of the College of Education, met with Favrot in New Orleans. The initial conversation must have taken Favrot by surprise. He recalled that they told him they "believe it is desirable to discontinue the San José Training School as an experimental school" at the end of the following session. The New Mexicans indicated to Favrot that the school would revert to the control of Bernalillo County. They explained that the reason for their decision was their inability to control enrollments at the school.[28] As a public, tax supported institution the school was required by law to take all students who lived in the district. Recent increases of the student body had severely hampered the research program and led to the decision to end the experiment.[29] In a "Proposed Reorganization of the San José Project," a plan written by Tireman and submitted later, it was requested that the final installment of GEB funds be spent on research projects involving statewide samples of Hispanic students.[30]

Before the New York board could respond to Tireman's first proposal another development changed the situation in New Mexico. Cyrus McCormick, Jr., scion of the International Harvester fortune, approached the university with a proposal of his own. He offered the university three thousand dollars a year for five years if it would undertake to provide social and educational help for the Hispanic village of Nambé near his home.[31]

Zimmerman immediately informed Nanninga and Tireman of the opportunity provided by the offer. Tireman was intrigued by the challenge and rewrote his proposal to the GEB and requested that unexpended funds be spent on the project in Nambé.[32] The revised proposal was approved by the GEB on June 2, 1937. The story of the reform of education in the state of New Mexico had moved its focus from San José to Nambé.

4
Nambé Community School: Origins and Community Health

The San José Demonstration and Experimental School was an enterprise that surely frustrated Tireman as well as provided him with some sense of success. The seven years spent planning and implementing the school were physically and emotionally very hard on the director and the faculty. Former teachers and staff recall the long, exhausting schedules that often included working late into the evening. The director seemed always to be there working as hard as the others.[1] Initially everyone was sustained by the hope that what they were doing at San José would help schools throughout the state and region. For Tireman, however, the experience at the San José school must have been disappointing in the final analysis. Always a person in a hurry, he allowed his hopes for the enterprise to obscure the hard, practical lessons learned as an administrator in Iowa.

He believed that the San José school would provide a beacon, a tangible example, that would quickly affect public schools and lead a parade of reform. His speeches and writing of the period communicate a kind of frustrated wonder that all could

64 Nambé

not see the simple solutions to the educational problems of rural and Hispanic children. Despite the letters telling Favrot that he was aware that educational reform would take decades, there remains the distinct impression that Tireman felt that his energy and dedication could significantly hurry the pace of reform.[2]

Faced with the loss of many of the talented professionals who had helped make the San José school a working and effective laboratory, continuing efforts there must have seemed fruitless. The planned research assessing the effectiveness of the San José program was disrupted and ultimately ruined by a rapidly changing school population.[3] Budget strains, and the loss of his administrative aides, occurred when Tireman's energy and interest were ebbing. The surprise is not that Tireman and Nanninga proposed ending the experiment at the San José school but that, considering the pressures and frustrations, they waited until 1937 to do it.

A picture of Tireman at San José at this time, when he was in his early forties, shows a man of medium height and thinning hair. A bulky jacket emphasizes his compact, strongly made torso. Looking straight at the camera, his slight smile emphasizes the determined set of his jaw. But as plans went forward to turn the San José school back to the Bernalillo County authorities, Loyd Tireman was tired, frustrated, but not defeated. Educational reform demanded his total energies, and he was to rise again to the challenge.

In spring 1937 another challenge was presented to him and, as always, for Tireman a challenge was an opportunity. Earlier in the year Cyrus McCormick, Jr., heir to the International Harvester fortune, had talked to President Zimmerman about securing help for the village of Nambé in northern New Mexico.[4]

In the early 1930s Mr. and Mrs. Cyrus McCormick, Jr. had

moved to northern New Mexico and built a large home. To add to their other landholdings in the area, they had purchased the site of the original Nambé school. In repayment for the land they gave a piece of land nearer the road to the community and the sum of one thousand dollars. By 1934 the McCormicks and the community had pooled their resources and constructed a new elementary school. The wealthy midwestern couple provided money for the construction project while the community provided the labor. This kind of cooperation was to be repeated many times in the future.[5]

When Cyrus McCormick, Jr. had approached President Zimmerman it is quite likely that he had had no trouble in getting an appointment. In his years in New Mexico, the magnate had become a strong political influence. He had organized a circle of friends who strongly influenced the rebuilding of the Republican party in the state. McCormick's money and political acumen had contributed to several successful campaigns. To further his political agenda and to serve the aim of encouraging creative writing in the region, he founded *The New Mexico Sentinel,* a weekly newspaper. As publisher McCormick set the editorial policy and wrote a regular column. The paper was unique in that it devoted, from 1937 on, a page to presenting the original work of southwestern writers.[6]

The McCormick couple was the largest landowner in the community of Nambé, just north of Santa Fe. They owned sixty-five acres contrasted with the average holding of four or five acres. Employment on the McCormick ranch was the most reliable source of money income locally and so was much prized. Involvement with the people of the village soon made McCormick and his wife aware of the social and medical problems of the village. In particular, they were concerned that the school in the community did not seem to be doing very much to help the villagers. What went on in the school did not appear to have much connection to health, nutrition, and general social needs of the Nambé people. As the problems of the people were intensified by the deepening economic depression that had begun in 1929, the couple's concerns became so strong that they were moved to contact the president of the university.[7]

McCormick offered Zimmerman three thousand dollars a year for five years if the University of New Mexico would provide community and educational aid to Nambé. Zimmerman immediately took the offer to Dean Nanninga and Tireman. Preliminary discussions rapidly progressed and produced an agreement between the McCormicks and the university. The Nambé public school would be fashioned into an instrument of social reform and community regeneration of the village. Tireman would direct the project. The new challenge energized the university professor and again provided him with an opportunity to construct an elementary education program that could serve as an example for the state and region.[8]

The Great Depression's impact had come late to New Mexico. But the deferred blow seemed to have gathered destructive energy. Unlike urban industrial and financial centers that had felt the impact very soon after the stock market and financial crash, rural regions of the country had had a grace period. Paradoxically, the financial backwardness and reliance on a more primitive barter economy had temporarily insulated these regions. For a few years, life seemed to go on undisturbed. However, when the collapse of the eastern stock and money markets, the closing of the great industrial factories, were finally felt in the small villages of northern New Mexico the impact was catastrophic. By the time the university, the McCormicks, and Tireman were involved with Nambé the traditional economy had collapsed, community institutions were in disarray, and survival itself was threatened.[9]

In 1937 the village of Nambé was comprised of a primarily Spanish-speaking population of 600 persons representing 160 families. Nambé was located about eighteen miles north of Santa Fe adjacent to Nambé Pueblo land. For more than two hundred years the Hispanic village had existed on the small Nambé river in usually friendly coexistence with the Pueblo.

In the village, cooperation was dictated by the continuing work required to maintain irrigation ditches. The ditches were crucial for growing of crops, hence communal self-help was a value based on long historical precedent. Indeed, one of the major irrigation ditches, built by the founder of the village, Gaspar Ortiz y Paiz, was aptly named "La Comunidad," characterizing it as the foundation of the community. This ditch is still in use.

To cooperation the villagers added the characteristic of stability. As late as the 1930s many of the families could claim direct blood kinship with the founder, Ortiz y Paiz. Slowly, however, even before the onset of the depression, the old values were being changed by circumstances beyond the control of the village. Ever since the middle of the previous century the requirements and attractions of a money economy had disrupted the traditional practices of bartering and exchanging farm produce for services.[10]

The gradual displacement of farming and ranching by wage work was greatly accelerated by the arrival of the railroads in northern New Mexico and southern Colorado. Building and operating the railroads provided many jobs. Mining and other enterprises associated with the extractive industries were encouraged by the availability of the railroads and, in turn, provided jobs. The First World War quickened the whole process of establishing a money market by creating new demands for produce and the means to bring the products back east.

Jobs and wages had changed the economy fundamentally by 1929. Records show that by that year, on the average, one person per family in the region went out to work for four to seven months for wages of from $40.00 to $100.00. At first this infusion of cash allowed Nambé to survive at the very time that traditional subsistence farming and ranching was failing.[11]

The catastrophic waves of the Great Depression eventually washed into the tiny village with devastating impact. A comprehensive survey of social conditions in the region done in 1935 by the United States Department of Agriculture documents the struggle to survive. The bare statistics convey something of the depth of despair that must have been felt in villages such as Nambé. "Today we find two or three working from communities that . . . sent out 100 to 150 each year. The net result is that . . . the relief load is between 60 and 70 percent of the people.[12] The same report adds that of those people not directly on relief most relied indirectly on relief support payments for a livelihood.

As the industrial prostration caused by the Great Depression spread and became a seemingly permanent condition, the survival hopes of communities in northern New Mexico appeared to depend upon the revivification of subsistence farming. Yet frustration met efforts to expand the old ways of farming. "Unscientific methods of agriculture" had greatly reduced fertility in the region. A great need, in addition to less wasteful methods of farming, was water for irrigation. However it was found that in the watershed of the Nambé River and other streams draining the region:

Deforestation and overgrazing in the upper reaches result in heavy floods and freshets in the early spring, with consequent heavy erosion. Practically all of the streams have carried down so much silt in recent years that the stream beds have become overloaded. The result is that floodwaters rechannel their course on either side of the original channel at floodtime, and thus destroy valuable farm land. This condition is not helped by the method of dividing the land that is prevalent in the area, which makes individual holdings into long, narrow strips extending from the upper irrigation ditches to the river, thus making effective terracing impossible.[13]

The report characterized the region as being "tragically overgrazed." There was a twofold reason for this condition: first, it was the net result of having perhaps five times more animals on the land than it could support. Second, the area had been afflicted by a drought since 1932. The government observers concluded "that the grass cover has been practically ruined and the animals left are literally 'skin and bones.'"

In human terms, by 1937 poverty in northern New Mexico was widespread and poor diet nearly universal. Surveys found that in some locales up to 90 percent of the children were undernourished. In more than a few cases medical investigators found chronic malnutrition among adults as well as children. In the resulting weakened condition all were vulnerable to infectious diseases as well as maladies resulting from vitamin deficiencies. Dangerous health conditions were intensified by ignorance of hygiene and both the shortage and pollution of water supplies. Public health clinics and education programs were urgently needed.[14]

Despite all of the negative findings, the government report concluded on a note of cautious optimism. It referred to the region as a "ready-made laboratory" in which to test different methods of economic and social recovery. Yet the optimism of the outside experts did not put food in the bellies of hungry children. People in small villages like Nambé must have despaired as they tried to deal with survival in a time of rapidly changing exigencies. Help was needed badly.[15]

As Tireman, after agreeing to be the director of the new project, walked through the community and tried to figure out what might be done to help, he came to a painful but not unanticipated conclusion. All of the evidence indicated that in Nambé the school had been functioning as a foreign, and irrelevant, imposition.

His ideas of this time were later distilled in a book, written with Mary Watson, school principal, about the experiences at Nambé. Discussing traditional American public school curriculum and its relevance to Hispanic communities, Tireman referred to the legend of the bed of Procrustes. He stated that public school curriculum was typically analogous to the legendary bed of the old robber. Schools forced children to fit the traditional "bed" of school subjects and, as a result, chopped off parts of some children and painfully stretched others to fit. Forcing youngsters into preordained levels and subjects reached extremes of inappropriateness with Spanish-speaking children. Hispanic children were expected to fit in with, and perform well in, a curriculum "originally designed for English-speaking children of the Atlantic seacoast."

Irrelevant instruction and the forcing of children into inappropriate "boxes" was happening at the time when, in the region and in the village of Nambé, the very fabric of life was endangered. Adults were without work, children were going hungry, and infants were sickening. "Yet," Tireman wrote, "the appalling fact is that the common school has helped very little." While government food programs, county nurses, and agricultural agents struggled against hunger, disease, and hopelessness, the local school stood outside the struggle, forcing "this lock-step-chain-gang called a class" to memorize irrelevancies.[16]

Tireman's intellectual vision of reform was influenced, perhaps formed, by the theories of the social reconstructionists, Lester Frank Ward, Albion W. Small, and George S. Counts. These theoreticians and popularizers held that schools and teachers were the potential rebuilders and reformers of society.[17] Typically, Tireman took abstract notions and applied them to the concrete problem at hand. Echoing the social reconstructionists and the progressives, he stated that anything done in the school had to be justified by the measure of social utility. "It is not recognized and honestly acknowledged that the curriculum could be and is an instrument of society and should be designed to do whatever needs to be done for the good of all."[18]

The social reconstruction agenda was, in the 1930s, energized by the wave of social melioration programs of the New Deal. By 1933 and 1934 programs to combat the social ills caused in part by the depression began to be available to New Mexicans. Tireman and the faculty of the Nambé Community School considered the school curriculum as an instrument that should be used to help the people with the problems that confronted them. Consequently, the school often became for the villagers a guide to deal with the confusing world of bureaucrats and acronyms.

For the McCormicks it is likely that one of the strong motivations for aiding Nambé was a kind of nostalgic desire to preserve Spanish village life. With this desire they joined Mary Austin and legions of other transplanted New Mexicans who imagined they saw in Hispanic rural life and art something that needed to be saved from urbanized and industrialized America.[19]

For Tireman the pragmatist the essence of the grand theories was that the school had to be useful. No part of what was done in the traditional school, no matter how hallowed by time and beloved by the faculty, had intrinsic value. A school had to help, had to be relevant. "A school should be the center of the community. It should be sensitive to the needs of the community and, in cooperation with the parents, plan a program that will make the best use of all available resources."[20]

This statement of "general philosophy" was anchored to practical ground at Nambé by a series of "principles of selection of subject matter." The principles were the final step in applying the abstractions of social reconstruction theory to the life of the Nambé Community School.

I. We shall try to find out what is most needed in the lives of the people of this community and minister to that before all else.
II. We shall constantly try to discover and utilize the resources of the community. The fields, arroyos, the homes, and the shops shall be a part of our laboratories, and its workers numbered among our teachers.
IV. The starting point in every part of the curriculum will be Nambe. . . .[21]

The first tasks of the director, principal, and faculty were to visit every home in the community and talk to the people about their problems and needs. The assessment of needs also allowed a list to be compiled of resources that might be used in the school. Home visits involved parents and community in the education of their children from the beginning and showed the adults that what would go on in the school was relevant to them.[22]

As the center of the community, the school had a reciprocal

relationship with its setting. Community problems influenced the content of the curriculum, and the school called on the community to provide resources (examples from the environment, skills of the artisans) to support its efforts. This interactive relationship between school and community is clearly illustrated in dealing with the health problems of Nambé.

Health conditions at Nambé were devastating in the 1930s. In this decade the infant mortality rate for the nation was 51 deaths for every 1,000 live births. In New Mexico at the same period the rate was almost 126. In some rural, predominantly Hispanic counties, 167 babies died out of every 1,000 live births.[23] In Nambé there were no medical facilities or regular service provided by a health professional. The nearest hospital was in Santa Fe and the closest medical doctor was in Española. The twenty-mile trip to either town involved traveling over dirt roads that soon became impassable in the winter or after the rains in the spring. Few villagers had dependable transportation or could afford the expense of the trip.[24]

In the village lack of hygienic training meant that dangerous conditions continued unchecked. Unscreened and untreated outdoor toilet facilities resulted in continuing contamination of food by flies. Largely because of unscreened homes, fly-carried disease was endemic, many children suffering from gastric distress, skin infections, or diarrhea. Polluted water supplies and a limited, poor diet due to poverty compounded the health problems of the community.

Health and hygiene conditions were identified as the major concern of the people of Nambé in the needs assessment done just before school opened. The director and the faculty made the health of the community and children the major focus of their efforts. Work was begun in the community by setting up a program of community health treatment and education. In the classrooms staying clean and well became one of the main organizing principles of lessons at all grade levels.[25]

Mrs. McCormick responded to the needs of the village by providing the money to hire a public health nurse. Tireman interviewed a woman for the position and her memory of the meetings verified that the man could be difficult. Maria Casias Vergara was working in northern New Mexico and heard about the job opening in Nambé. Young, well-trained, and motivated by a strong desire to help the rural people, she donned her best clothes and journeyed to Nambé. The interview did not last long. When Tireman saw the attractive, well-dressed young woman, he dismissed her with the abrupt comment that he was not interested in hiring "movie stars." Startled by the rebuke, she was silent, but soon she recovered and returned to Nambé. This time she wore her work clothes, and her knowledge and determination won her the job. Aware of his manner, she later stood up to the intimidating professor and told him to leave the health program to her; he could handle the education program.

Apparently Tireman's intuition led him to use interviews as tests. If a person seeking a job could stand up to him, then it was likely that that person was strong and confident enough to deal with the rigors of working in an experimental school setting. This hiring method was particularly successful when it brought Maria Casias Vergara into the project. She was familiar with the area and was a seemingly inexhaustible source of ideas and energy as she organized the community health program and advised teachers on the curriculum. School faculty assisted her in the community work.[26]

Improving community health began with efforts to raise the nutritional level of the people's diet. Because winter meals often lacked vegetables and fruits, the county extension service brought in a home demonstration agent to teach the women to can and dry fruits and vegetables. More healthful methods of handling food, covering leftovers and not overcooking food, were also taught by the agent.

School staff helped to improve children's diets by initiating a midmorning snack for the younger children. Milk was obtained from the WPA and supplemented with fruit, crackers, cereal, or surplus commodities available through other New Deal agencies. Parents eagerly supported the efforts to improve their children's food intake. They brought food donations of cabbages, potatoes, and carrots from their winter stores. The McCormicks contributed vegetables, apples, and milk for the nursery school. During the winter months it was not uncommon to find a box of apples in every room.

The mid-morning snack was continued until the last two years of the project when the WPA, after much urging by Tireman and Watson, established a hot lunch project in Nambé. During the last two years of the project, a kitchen staff of five served a hot, well-balanced meal to the children of the upper and lower schools.[27]

By early 1939 ad hoc groups of parents organized a formal Health Committee made up of ten community people, the nurse, and the principal. The monthly meetings of this group served to spread information, since some of the sessions were made up of lectures on child health and community hygiene. Meeting agendas often dealt with active involvement of the lay people in helping their children.

During the first year of the committee's organization over $140 was raised through movies, benefit dances, plays, and contributions. The money was used for tonsillectomies, glasses, dental work, flannel for layettes, and the construction of a sanitary privy for the church. The improvement of the toilet facilities at the church had wide benefits since the clean,

76 Nambé

screened rest rooms were a symbol and illustration of scientific hygiene noted by the whole community.[28]

The nurse and the committee greatly benefited the health practices of the community. In classrooms, as well, important lessons in personal hygiene were being learned.

> The children became health conscious. . . . The school rooms supported the health program by providing situations in which the children could learn and experience practices of good health. . . . They washed their hands before lunch. They washed their hands when they returned from the toilet. They went to lunches of well-cooked food served on tables set with napkins and silverware and clean, individual dishes. They learned to eat foods they were not used to, first because these foods were good for them and later because they liked them. They learned to eat and demand fruit juices, vegetables, and green salads. They rested regularly, they drank quantities of milk, ate whole wheat bread—and they gained weight![29]

Classrooms supported the nurse's work by providing situations in which students could learn about and use good health practices. Younger children, with the help of their teachers, composed short essays detailing their experiences with proper food, safety, controlling flies, cleanliness, and personal hygiene. In the upper grades, there were microscopes for testing well and river water. The children studied sanitation and wells, the causes of disease, proper foods, and means of preventing illness and providing good health.[30]

Children were constantly encouraged to see the class lessons as practical exercises. That they understood the message is clear from an incident that involved the fourth and fifth graders. They had been studying water and sanitation and causes of illness. They observed the digging of a well located on a slope below some toilets on private land. Worried about the implications of such a project they informed the teacher. After discussing different steps to take, a committee was appointed who found out from the owner that the toilets were to be removed. The health of the family was protected and the children in the fourth and fifth grades received an invaluable lesson in community action and responsibility.[31]

Though there were instances when old habits stymied the health program, it was generally successful. The teachers and the nurse were effective in changing the health practices of the community. The success, however, was not due solely to the efforts of these adults. Children were often the most effective advocates in the community of the new programs of health and hygiene. Anecdotes abound of youngsters urging their mothers to use hygienic methods in the home, to cover food, and get rid of flies. A six year old, Gloria, refused to drink water from a glass recently used by her sick sister thereby giving her parents a practical, and probably successful, lesson in germ theory.[32]

Soon after coming to the community the nurse inspected all of the children's teeth. Finding extensive evidence of lack of dental care, she launched a "toothbrush campaign." Discussions at the Health Committee meetings and in classrooms soon convinced children that they should brush regularly. Sons and daughters carried the message to the home and soon storekeepers were having to lay in new supplies of toothbrushes and toothpaste.[33]

Since the school had no well, children had to carry water in pails from their homes and store the pails in the classroom for use through the day. Such an arrangement involved a great deal of trouble and provided many opportunities for contamination. In 1940 a Well Committee organized at the urging of the school undertook to raise money for a well. The principal, Mary Watson, records how she and Cordelia Ortiz, the pre-first class teacher, "went calling" throughout the village to collect donations for the well. Their mission was a success since they collected many donations, but more money was needed. Within a few months, at a meeting of the Well Committee, a prominent community member donated land near the school for the well and storage tank. It was established at the meeting that money was only needed for the tank and pipes, each man volunteered to help dig the well. In the summer of 1941 the well was completed and the availability of fresh water in the school constituted another step in the health and unity of the village of Nambé. The successful digging of the well epitomizes the success of the school program in promoting health and hygiene.[34]

5
Nambé Community School: Curriculum and Conservation

Dealing with community problems often required organizing new, de facto committees. The urgency of the problems, especially health and nutrition concerns, favored setting up single or limited purpose action groups. Both the Health and the Well Committees were examples of limited purpose groups. But if the community of Nambé were to survive the Depression, it would have to learn new ways of relating within the community and outside. The Community School had to help existing social institutions in Nambé work out new ways of relating to each other as well as to outside agencies.

The school, the Parent-Teacher Association, and the fraternal group/union (the Mutual Protective Society of United Workers or SPMDTU) were institutions that antedated Tireman and the Community School. As Tireman's judgment of the previous school at Nambé attests, however, the village school had done little to help the community deal with its problems. Before Tireman the school had been in the village but had not been a part of it. The PTA had only recently been reorganized and was not yet an effective influence. The

SPMDTU membership was made up of men who could afford to pay the membership dues. Effectiveness in aiding its membership was limited, and by 1937 the union's slender financial resources had been depleted by the depression. Before the Community School it is likely that the three organizations existed alongside each other with few formal or reciprocal contacts. Cooperation and exchange among them was probably incidental if it did occur.[1]

However, with the Community School acting as the catalyst, the SPMDTU and the PTA gained new vigor and a deeper understanding of the need for cooperation. Meetings of the newly reconstituted PTA at the school became opportunities for parents (typically the mothers) to learn about committee organization and school finances, and to plan educational and health activities. The mothers' direct involvement in the care and health of their families was strengthened at the meetings where they learned what they might do to keep their charges well. Women who were unskilled in organizational matters and perhaps reticent in discussion and debate were "schooled" at first in the PTA in conversations about immediate housekeeping matters. Confidence gained in such conversations soon led PTA members into more positive, initiating activities.

PTA meetings were usually chaired—in fact if not in title—by Mary Watson. Under her sensitive direction and tutelage, often assisted by Maria Casias or Cordelia Ortiz, the women soon learned how to organize to deal with a problem. It became a habit for them to look to the school for help.[2] In a similar way the men of the SPMDTU were impressed by the help the Community School was giving the village in soil conservation and animal husbandry. The school modeled the behavior it wished to encourage among the institutions in the community.

Soon after the school opened in the fall of 1937, two union

representatives approached the principal with a request. Tentatively and respectfully, probably testing her commitment to the recently stated tenets of the Community School, the men asked for assistance in organizing some entertainment at the annual meeting of the SPMDTU. Their doubts disappeared when Mary Watson, quite characteristically, replied by asking them how long a program they wanted.

The annual union celebration was a great success. Teachers were able to show the community what was being done in the school through the performances of their students. Parents got a chance to proudly watch their children on stage. The school's cooperation so impressed the SPMDTU members that, two months after the celebration, another deputation from the union visited Mary Watson. They informed her that the membership had voted to allow the school free use of the union hall anytime for school activities.[3]

By helping them, the school had affected both village institutions and had changed their relationship to one another. Responding to the school's example of cooperation, the PTA and SPMDTU were soon sponsoring health drives to get the children's teeth examined and to have all newborns given checkups by the nurse. The two organizations supported and helped the school organize an annual School Day to publicize the children's work and the school program. Together they raised money for projects and donated food to the school snack and lunch activities.[4]

Tireman had written during the organizing period of the school that the faculty would find out what was most needed in the lives of the people of Nambé and minister to those needs before all else. Relevance to village life was a fundamental goal of the Community School, and in the list of principles guiding the curriculum it was stated that:

The starting point in every part of the curriculum will be Nambé. The pupil may go to the farthest point of the earth but he must follow the plan of going from something that is familiar and well known to something that is over the horizon. Unless that connection can be established by the pupils, we will relentlessly omit that part of the curriculum no matter how sanctified it may be by tradition and academic respectability.[5]

The organization of the Community School embodied these abstract notions. Classroom activities, field trips, everything that happened in school and in the village, was utilized to meet the goal of relating what the child knew and immediately experienced to the wider world. Relevance meant that the school responded to the needs enunciated by the people of the village, and the health program was an example of that response. Readiness to help and to utilize immediate experience as a gateway to the world and abstract ideas was also evident in the school's work with land fertility, soil conservation, landownership, and irrigation.

The 1937 needs assessment had identified health and agriculture as the two most prominent concerns of the people of Nambé. Land problems were intensified during the years of the Community School's operation. Despite a history of peaceful coexistence between the Pueblo and village, legality of landownership became a problem in the 1920s and later. An enormously complex Indian Pueblo Lands Controversy beginning at this time had thrown into doubt the land claims of many rural Hispanic people. Tempers and fears had reached such intensity that armed incidents had occurred in Nambé in 1922–23.[6]

The only faculty member who was a native of the village was aware of the difficult position of her people and urged the school to educate the community in the complexities of legal landownership. The teacher wrote that "most of the [Spanish] people had no idea that they needed any kind of documents about land purchased." She went on to say, "many of the farms were taken away from Spanish people and giving [sic] them back to the Indians."[7] In response the school emphasized the importance of legally established titles of ownership. Teachers and government advisors urged parents to collect their deeds of ownership so that they might prove continuous ownership since 1900 and so hold on to their land.[8]

Agricultural problems went beyond the substantial difficulties of proving landownership; education for improved land use was also needed. Another teacher, a native New Mexican Hispanic, wrote that "if this or any other Spanish community is to exist or ever hope to maintain a decent standard of living, they've got to be taught the value" of scientific cultivation. He went on to say that wasteful methods of farming were "Nambé's basic problem." With training in better methods of farming the people could enjoy a higher standard of living.[9] As it was to do often, the Community School identified sources of help within the burgeoning federal bureaucracy and recruited aid from the agencies. By means of the Emergency Education Act, expert agricultural aid for training of adults was secured through the Federal Emergency Relief Administration (FERA) and the Works Progress Administration (WPA). Agronomists from the Soil Conservation Service were also recruited to lend their help to the Nambé villagers.

Even more important than the immediate help in farming and conserving soil fertility were the classes in literacy. Generally supported by the WPA and organized by the school, classes in adult literacy came to the village. Reading and writing in English meant that the people of Nambé could hope to deal successfully with the complexities of a rapidly growing state and federal government.[10]

Agricultural training in the school and community followed three simple, but crucial, principles of curriculum development. 1) When students were given a problem to deal with they were encouraged to interrelate disciplines. Traditional boundaries between subject matter were to disappear. 2) Problems might first be discussed in the local and immediate context, but concerns were to be directed to the wider connections beyond Nambé. 3) Students were to be encouraged to be involved and to use their minds and experiences by the use of discussion, questioning, evaluation, and critical thinking.

Again, Tireman summed up the approach in the following manner:

we decided to emphasize health and land management. Throughout the various grades we would attempt to impregnate the regular subjects with concepts from these two fields. Thus, as far as we could, we would use reading materials which discussed these topics. Our social science work was centered around their ramification, e.g., relation of the proper use of land to prosperity of "all of us"; the effect of a good health program upon "La Comunidad." Some of our arithmetic problems could deal with actual problems in Nambé.[11]

With Tireman and Watson, the faculty translated the general notion into a curriculum plan for every grade. The following outline prepared after the tenure of the Community School gives a general idea of how the plan was translated into activities in the classroom.

Pre-first grade—Specific concentrations on school acquaintances, pets, the home, and the garden; special emphasis on acquiring a beginning functional English vocabulary of 500–750 words; stress on practicing basic health and cleanliness habits.

First grade—Studied foods of Nambé, growing pets and pet care, garden life, insect and animal life of Nambé; special emphasis on beginning instruction in reading, tied to a natural science program and a terrarium.
Second and third grades—Flowers and gardening studied on alternate years; also studies of individuals who contributed to make Nambé a more pleasant and better place to live for all; bird life and domestic animals were studied in alternate years; special class trips were taken to observe the activities of the community and group discussions and group compositions were participated in afterwards.
Fourth and fifth grades—Studied irrigation. Water, the land, and man as interdependent, first at Nambé, then in the broader contexts of the state, the Southwest and the country.
Sixth and seventh grades—Concentrated on a study of how to keep records; also on animals and plants of the earth, and man and the world he lives in; individual and group projects were encouraged, with special emphasis on oral discussion and group compositions which could then be used as reference material for all.
Eighth grade—Specific concentrations on the Second World War, and on conserving the land; much work stressing group cooperation and individual responsibility, doing individual research and bringing it together for the benefit of all; special emphasis on the balance of nature and studying the problems of Nambé through asking such questions as "How are standards of living related to the land? Why is the land around Nambé so eroded? What can be done to prevent erosion and correct it? Do plants and animals have anything to do with erosion? What are good crops for Nambé farmers to plant?"[12]

Clearly, general plans do not give a sense of the human interaction, a flavor of what went on in the classrooms. Some teachers were undoubtedly more adept at acting in a serendipitous fashion, taking advantage of unanticipated opportunities to develop an important theme introduced by students. Some teachers probably felt more comfortable staying close to a prepared lesson. A diary entry describes a class session among seventh and eighth graders and gives valuable insight into how one teacher used methods of question and discussion to direct students from consideration of an immediate question to one with broader implications.

The B group in the circle had already begun to check their seatwork by reading sections from the book to prove their answers. When I went up Matilde was heatedly defending her answer. In discussion, we traced the routes of the Spanish and English pioneers. I asked, "why didn't the Spanish explorers destroy as much of the natural resources as the English explorers?" Manuel said they had. This led us into a discussion which brought in factors of surface, climate, purposes of early colonists, use of land and its effect upon people today. As Angelita put it, "They weren't thinking of us." I asked, "Do you think people who settled in Nambé thought of future generations?" The children agreed that perhaps they hadn't and this brought us to the question, "What about us? Are we thinking about future generations?" Irene, who had been on a community land-use investigating committee last year, brought up the point of the amount of land and the increasing population and the practice of dividing land among heirs. Pita said, "If the land is poor, poor crops are raised and people don't have enough money to buy things they need." I prodded, "What are young people growing up now to do? Will they all live here in the valley?" As recess time was near I asked if they would like to keep on with the discussion. They were all interested in doing so and I asked if we could phrase a topic which we could keep in mind. We all agreed to think over and discuss for next time "Problems of Land Use in

Nambé." We were to jot down all of the ideas we could think of as well as ask our parents for the ones they thought important.[13]

By the adroit use of questions this teacher was able to help the students move from the textbook abstractions and a discussion of the early explorers to assessment of land use in their village. Students were reminded of the pattern of landownership when Irene contributed her information. This led them to consider their own possible future in the village. An invaluable lesson was learned as a result of the development of Angelita's insight: humans do not act responsibly in dealing with the ecology, present generations do not seem to worry very much about the future of the land and environment. The girl's observation would seem to be appropriate fifty years later. The teacher wisely kept the valuable discussion open for future sessions and encouraged students to get their parents involved.

Wise use of natural resources was constantly and practically emphasized in the Community School. Protection from land erosion and improvement of grazing land was taught when students fenced off a section of land, planted it in grass donated by the Soil Conservation Service Agent, and compared the planted segment with land that was open for grazing. Such demonstration projects were surely observed closely by fathers as well as the students involved. Even unobservant parents were perhaps drawn into discussions of the interrelated problems of ground cover and erosion by their children of school age.[14]

Balance in nature and rotation of crops was taught in practical ways in a garden that was planted on the school grounds. In addition, the McCormicks donated an acre of land to the school and this donation was prepared and planted by the students with some voluntary help from several men. The land was planted in "peas, radishes, and beets," and was surely the motivation for a great deal of student interest and learning.[15]

As with the health program, instruction of students in improved methods of agriculture made them excellent ambassadors and agents of reform in their own homes. A boy in the upper school reported to his teacher that he had talked his father out of burning off the grass and weeds that grew along the ditchbanks. He reported that he had explained to his father that the vegetation held the soil and burning would encourage erosion. That the parent heeded his son is evidence of the youngster's salesmanship as well as the respect the parent had for the source of his son's information.[16]

Adults in the community grew more and more ready to see the school as a sympathetic source of help and information. When a schoolboy's father was preparing to expand his orchard, the child was sent to school with a request for information. A booklet on the proper preparation and cultivation of fruit trees was found and sent home. Later there was further aid from the County Extension Agent on a visit to the orchard arranged by the school.[17]

The Community School provided aid to the village by acting as organizer and coordinator of the services offered by other agencies. By the time the Nambé Community School became active, the generalized desire to help people, to alleviate the ills of the Great Depression, that characterized the New Deal had resulted in many federal programs. Though these federal programs were instituted to help people, their record of relief was very spotty. Proud and independent farmers and ranchers of Nambé were not used to looking outside the village to the government for help. Surely the welter of acronyms, bureaucrats, rules and forms was intimidating and often seemed invasive.[18]

In their book written after the Nambé experiment, Tireman

and Watson described the ideal position the Community School ought to occupy between community and government agency:

> The functional program of the community school was dependent upon the assistance of the numerous agencies and organizations. Without the interest and understanding of the individuals who represented the various agencies many phases and achievements of the program would have been impossible. The greatest value of the program of the cooperating agencies is that the use of their services was not unique to Nambé. It was the utilization of the resources which are available to every public school in the country, if the staff is willing to contact these agencies and use the assistance they are able to give. Yet such a service program cannot succeed unless the people have been awakened to the need of such help.[19]

The Community School secured help from the Forest Service, the WPA, the National Youth Administration, and the Soil Conservation Service most often. Educational materials for the land use program were provided by the Forest Service. Later, the same agency cut and trimmed the large roof timbers (vigas) for the woodworking shop. The WPA helped the school most immediately by funding the school hot lunch program and providing a recreational leader for exercise sessions. The same agency gave employment to some of the community, helped fund some of the construction on school additions, and helped set up the nursery school in 1938. The NYA employed some of the older youths in the community to help in the school. The building of the woodworking shop and providing a teacher for the same shop was due to the efforts of the NYA also. The Soil Conservation Service provided the teaching services of their agents. Pamphlets and seeds were also provided by the SCS agents.[20]

The Community School recruited and utilized state agencies as well. Often state services were underwritten by federal monies and provided another set of bewildering rules and services that the school helped the community deal with. The State Health Department aided in the establishment and support of the extensive health program administered by Maria Casias. The Extension Service of the New Mexico State Agricultural College provided agricultural agents and home demonstration agents to instruct in the care of gardens and preservation of food, establishing a 4H and Nature Study Club, and organizing vocational training projects. The State Library in Santa Fe helped set up a library program in Nambé and provided much of the recreational literature used by children and adults.[21]

In particular, one County Extension Agent, Fabiola C. de Baca Gilbert, whose work was facilitated by the school, was especially helpful to the girls of Nambé. She organized the Girls's 4H Club and visited the school twice a month on a regular basis to advise and assist the teachers and the girls.[22]

The spontaneous nature of some of the visits indicates that the faculty welcomed the visits and the government functionaries viewed the contacts as more than just work. Mary Watson recorded that "At 1:15 who should come by but Miss Ann Raymond. She gave the pupils a very interesting talk on Soil Conservation." Another government employee traveled to Nambé on his day off and provided information that strengthened in Watson's mind the need for a locally relevant curriculum:

Mr. Musgrave and wife came Sunday and brought a splendid citrus exhibit from his home in Phoenix. . . . He made an interesting statement about the citrus fruits. It seems that the early Spanish Friars brought the buds and seeds with them when they came on their early journeys to the New World. Here is another reason for teaching history from the Southern or Spanish entrance rather than from the English point of view.²³

In the quoted passage Mary Watson quite evidently shares the often repeated views of the Community School director on relevance. For almost fifteen years Tireman had been reiterating his observation that the lack of interest shown by Spanish-speaking children in school was due to their confusion and the irrelevance of the curriculum. The children were unable "to see any connection between the material they are studying and their life outside school." The gap and the resulting ennui and disengagement largely disappeared when lessons were interesting and connected to the children's life.²⁴

Tireman and the school faculty correctly observed that survival and a fuller, healthier life in the future required that the people of Nambé become more sohisticated in dealing with government and its agencies:

The children realized the importance of the agencies and were fully aware of their existence. The people realized that the agencies existed for their use. By constant effort on the part of the teaching staff and the individuals who represented the agencies a groundwork was established that we hoped would not be destroyed when the project was ended. A way was opened for the people to make the best use of community and state resources. . . .²⁵

Connection of the expanding state and federal government to the life of the village was the tactic used to help the children realize the importance of the agencies. Examples of the application of the idea of relevance to the curriculum abound in the diaries of the teachers. The following excerpt shows how a distinctive vegetable, the chile pepper, was used to help the children learn writing and letter composing.

> Children have written recipes for chile. The other day we were writing up recipes and in our discussion we finally led up to a dandy lesson in sequential thinking on how to make "chile caribe." I thought it would be something very valuable. To make a booklet with our finding on chile to send to parents [sic]. Have written letters to Mr. Ramirez, Catalog Co's, State College, County Agents. Will write to Arizona, California, Burbank Farms, Texas, Mexico for more information on chile. Children are getting to be good letter writers. We are realizing our great need for correct spelling, good English and paragraph organization.[26]

Using an item that was so close to their lives to help teach English skills meant that intrinsic motivation among the children was likely to be high. The enthusiasm the children felt in penning letters to far away places must have partially overcome the tediousness of writing in a somewhat unfamiliar language. The arbitrary rules of letter writing and English orthography were probably offset for the pupils by the prospect of producing a booklet for their parents.

Applying lessons learned at San José, teachers led classes on walks through Nambé visiting the local store, grist mill, or garage and providing a rich source of material for later use in the classroom. Returning from their walks the children would eagerly discuss what they had seen and develop their thoughts about their observations. Often the teacher would develop from the children's discussions "reading charts" for later use as a "supplement to the more conventional reading program." Following are some examples of the reading charts.

Ernesto's shoes—Ernesto has some new shoes. His father made them Saturday. He worked all day. They are made of leather. The soles are made of cowhide. The tops are made of deerskin.[27]

The occupations important in the life of the village provided an important source of information for classroom discussion. The children observed that:

The baker—The baker works all day in the bakery. He takes care of the machinery that makes the good bread and cakes we like. He wears a clean, white suit every day. He keeps his bakery clean so we will buy his bread.
The garage man—The garage man sells oil, gasoline, and tires for cars. He repairs automobiles and trucks when they break. He greases our cars and trucks so they will run better and last longer.[28]

The use of local resources in the English and reading programs in the classroom also involved support of the health program. Visiting the nurse was an occasion to learn about her work and public health.

The nurse—The nurse helps us. She puts bandages on us when we have a cut or a sore. The nurse vaccinates us so we will not have smallpox. She is a kind friend.
The fly—The fly is very dirty. Flies carry many diseases. Flies like to live in dirty places. We should keep our homes clean so that flies will not live in them. We should have screens on our doors and windows.[29]

Finally, reading charts were developed to help children who were having a great deal of difficulty reading. These charts often used natural history and agricultural topics.

Litter—There is ground litter under the trees. There is usually some litter under the bushes. This litter helps to hold the moisture in the ground. It helps the rain and snow to go down to the water table. People and plants get water from the water table. *Different vegetables*—At the Nambe Fair we saw plants which many of us do not raise. Not all of us raise citron, eggplant, cauliflower, and summer squash. A good kind of preserves is made from citron, lemons, and sugar. Eggplant is very good peeled, sliced thin, dipped in beaten egg, and fried. Cauliflower is cooked in boiling salted water. Summer squash is white and scalloped, and is cooked just like yellow squash.[30]

The younger students made clay models of farms depicting animals common to them and implements used. The manipulative play provided practice in language since the teacher encouraged the youngsters to talk about their models and explain what was happening on the farm. Showing and telling was an opportunity for the children to use English as well as a chance for the teacher to evaluate progress and identify areas that needed more practice.[31]

Seventh and eighth graders often used field trips to carry out science investigations. Such science projects typically involved problems of local interest. In one project water from the Nambé River and from the ditches was collected by the older students. The specimens were brought back to the classroom and analyzed.

The river water had 1% silt to the gallon. The ditch water had 13% to the ½ gallon. Arturo and Viola instantly said, "Why, sure. We have to clean the ditches of silt every year." Joe D. said, "Well, if one farmer sods his ditch and terraces his land so the soil won't go off into the ditch, it won't do any good. The other farmers don't do it." I broached, "How can this problem be solved, then?" Longino reluctantly said, "I guess each farmer will have to do his part." "But what about the silt in the river?" Epimenio, whose father has cattle in the mountains, ventured, "I know, my father sells cows. He make [sic] a lot of money if he raises a lot of cattle. But many cattle on the upper watershed, overgraze the land and the soil comes down."[32]

The lesson involving the silting of the irrigation ditches taught mathematics and erosion as well as the importance of the intangibles of cooperation and interdependence. In particular, young Epimenio discovered a fundamental economic dilemma that continues to trouble farmers and ranchers. Agriculture, animal husbandry, even the care and feeding of pets provided rich sources of material for classroom work. Anything bearing on the lives of the children, their parents and the village in general was raw material for the classroom. Tireman made the point that:

A community school must not be satisfied to confine its work to the school grounds. It must extend the walls of the classrooms to embrace any part of the community which can contribute something of value to the school program.[33]

Decisively rejecting the traditional notion of a school as something existing in but not a part of the community, the professor described how the more traditional pedagogical tools fit into the active community curriculum.

The experiences of the residents are freely called up to supplement the more conventional reading materials. This conception of a curriculum makes the textbook but one tool, as is proper. It utilizes in the school room the other agencies of education which are ordinarily relegated to the hours outside of the school room. Where it is impossible to visit the parents who have some specialized knowledge of value, they are brought to the school. The more carefully the resources of the community are listed, the more apparent it is that therein lies a wealth of material which ordinarily we do not tap.[34]

At the annual Nambé Fairs students and teachers showed the community the results of work done in the classrooms. Parents as well were encouraged to show their handicrafts and garden produce. Entries were judged and ribbons were awarded. These recreational fairs stressed the important lessons of practical learning, relevance, and reciprocal relations between community and school.[35]

In 1938 and 1939, the Community School neared the height of its success. Accepted by the village and respected by government agencies, the school had worked out a curriculum that was both relevant and effective. Success created additional needs when it was determined that the village would benefit from the construction of a woodworking shop. The shop would be associated with the school, and would provide needed employment for unemployed men and older boys. In addition, the shop could be used by the community to build furniture and other items that would improve health and the quality of life.

The construction project was a cooperative venture involving the men who volunteered to make or lay adobes and the women who volunteered to plaster the walls. One teacher reported a degree of community eagerness that conceivably interfered with the regular procedures of the school day.

The interest in the new building is very evident. . . . Mr. Garduno and Mr. Rael, both workers at McCormicks, stopped me on the way to school to ask if they could send some workers to help in the construction of the new building. They both sent some. Amabé, one of the young men of the community, also asked if he could come to help. Joe A. Romero asked if he could come to help on Saturdays. He goes to high school during the week. Mr. Sandoval, the P.T.A. president, sent or is to send a man over to work for him; he works on the highway. All are planning to use the new shop.[36]

The Forest Service provided the wooden support beams for the roof (vigas), while the school provided the windows and hardware. The NYA provided the instructor.

Once construction of the shop was complete it was soon being used continuously. Furniture, baby cribs, screen windows, and doors were among the most popular items made in the woodworking facilities. Very soon it was clear that the original shop needed to be enlarged. Most of the work on the addition was done by men who had learned their woodworking skills in the original shop. The woodshop provided the means for the community to help itself and so embodied the very best of the goals of the Community School.[37]

Sadly, a few years later, in the summer of 1942, the Nambé Community School came to an end. At a community meeting the village of Nambé voted to return the elementary school to the jurisdiction of the Santa Fe School District. This action was taken despite Cyrus McCormick's offer to continue his support of the experimental school. The reasons for the vote to end the Community School are complex and even obscure, but the following influences seem to be plausible explanations for the action.[38]

The declaration of war in late 1941 drew the leaders of the educational reform effort into government service. At the same time that the school lost most of its key leadership, most of the younger and, probably, more liberal villagers left the community to join the armed forces or to seek employment in the rapidly expanding war industries.

Though the war was disruptive and undoubtedly added to the social strains in the village, it does not seem to have been the main factor in closing the school. According to available reports, as the time approached for the community to reconsider its original mandate, a great deal of fear and anger was voiced by some citizens. Anger arose from a feeling that the school had not done what it had promised to do. Since some parents believed the school had failed, they feared for their children's chances in an increasingly dangerous and rapidly changing world. As happens so often in controversies over school reform, the Nambé School program was accused of being soft and undemanding. Complex feelings and issues became simplified into charges of neglect that probably arose from the differences between the old and new, between school experiences of the parents and those of the children. The Community School was accused of neglecting student discipline and homework. The teaching of the Spanish language and singing Spanish songs seemed to Spanish-speaking parents, who had confronted prejudice in the larger society, to be attempts to keep the children in an inferior, depressed status.

By contrast, one observer, an Anglo inhabitant of Nambé in the 1940s, said that the Nambé villagers felt "woodworking was all right, but they wanted the boys back on the farms—to do the farms. They wanted the girls in the kitchen." This villager has described the classic and wrenching dilemma of parents in a rural setting. Two probably universal and conflicting wishes for their children contended in these parents: the desire that children enjoy more opportunities than their parents did; and the desire that their children remain at home. Apprehension for their children fueled the controversy. Parents demanded goals that were impossible for the Nambé School, or any other school, to realize and this meant that the outcome was inevitable.[39]

There seemed to be some support for the criticisms and fear of the community. Claims were made that Nambé students did not do well when they went to the high school in Pojoaque. One community member recalled a dramatic incident in which a father brought his son to a community meeting. The father claimed that his son had attended the Community School for some years and could neither read nor add.[40]

Was this and other incidents effective political campaigning or evidence that the school had failed? How much was rumor and how much fact? Of course, these questions cannot be answered clearly now and may not have been answerable in the 1940s. The "truth" lies not in an exact rendering of events— an impossible task now—but in trying to figure out how humans involved in the events felt and what motivated them. Clearly, the opponents of the Community School feared for their children. Representing what might be termed the school faction, a Nambé teacher claims that students from the village did not do well in high school because they were bored. the Nambé program had been effective, and its success contributed to its termination!

The vote on the continuation of the school had really been decided earlier when a young man named Frank Lopez had returned to his home in Nambé. Lopez had been studying education at the University of Chicago and earned an M.A. degree.[41] As a man raised in the area, Lopez was to devote his life to education and helping improve the life of his people. Active in area politics, he eventually became superintendent of Pojoaque schools.

Forceful, influential, and brimming with new ideas from his graduate school tenure, Lopez smarted no doubt from his awareness of the neglect and condescension with which his people were being treated.[42] To him the Community School must have seemed an embodiment of Anglo-inspired prejudice, of cultural colonizing. A Nambé teacher recalls that Frank Lopez "thought they [Nambé Community School] were teaching them [students] to stay in the community and not giving enough attention to the skills of math and so forth."[43]

The village faction that criticized the school for not encouraging youngsters to stay at home, and the faction that faulted the school for not preparing students to join the national job market, both found a leader in Frank Lopez. Contradictory, though very human, sets of complaints arose, probably from the amorphous and unfocused fears of change and vague apprehensions about the future. The factions organized and ably led by Lopez seemed to be primarily motivated by fears of change. The depression had forever modified the basic sense of independence enjoyed in the past by the villagers. The widening carnage in Europe and the Pacific drew young men away to the military, and whole families left the village to pursue the promise of high pay in defense industries. Nothing could be done to change the national forces intruding in Nambé, but the villagers could insure that they knew what was going on in their children's school by forcing a return to traditional education, the kind of school they had attended.

Paradoxically the cultural portion of the school program aided Frank Lopez's campaign to end the Community School. The school emphasized cultural awareness and pride. With the success of the school program there was a growing sense of sophistication, confidence, and competency in the village in dealing with the burgeoning federal and state government. No doubt when Lopez returned to his home he was able to focus disenchantment in the village on an institution largely conceived and managed by outsiders.[44]

Did success end the Nambé Community School?[45] An interesting and important question; probably one that can not be answered. Reforming, making more progressive, an institution that is essentially a conserving and maintaining one is a difficult task at best. The initial successes of the Community School grew out of immediate and dire need. In the depths of the depression, when people were starving and children dying from lack of basic medical care, the Nambé School filled a clear need every day when it served a hot lunch. In a hundred other ways the school helped and, as long as need was painfully apparent and immediate, received community support.

As the suffering eased, attitudes changed. New Deal programs took effect and there was food, some jobs, and a little money. War brought more jobs and opportunities as it disrupted the community by enticing people to the big cities where the jobs were. Survival ceased to loom large and people began to look to the future with optimism. Of course, the future was the children and, in the midst of flux, the people became increasingly concerned for their children's prospects.

It would be wrong to interpret the termination of the school as an example of "betrayal," short-sightedness, or lack of gratitude by the villagers. Real people interacted every day for more than five years.[46] Dry ideas and theories cannot convey the slowly growing disaffection among people who start a relationship as friends. Prejudices among educators and villagers alike magnified thoughtlessness into major insult. Minor discourtesies, perhaps due to weariness or cultural ignorance, grew into major breaches of trust.[47]

Perhaps schooling is always to some degree a tussle between institution and parental love. School, as society's tool of separation of the child from the family, attempts to entice the child into society by dangling rewards, while parents try to hang on. Time favors the goals of the school, but the struggle continues.

With the ending of the Nambé Community School the experimental school programs developed and directed by Tireman came to an end. His reform work, however, continued.

During the war years he was involved most of the time in traveling through South America advising governments on educational program change and reform.[48] His vitality remained phenomenal and during this period he published *La Comunidad*, the story of the Nambé School he wrote with Mary Watson. He also began his *Mesaland Series* of readers for young children.[49]

In 1946 he served as the elementary education expert on the staff of the Washington State School Survey. When the Washington State project was completed he was approached by the federal government and asked to work for them again. Tireman went to Bolivia under the aegis of the Office of the Inter-American Affairs to help reorganize that nation's system of normal schools. Later he was the head of the United States delegation to the International Conference on Illiteracy held in Rio de Janeiro.[50] An important result of this work in Latin America was that groups of South American educators traveled north to the University of New Mexico to attend seminars and receive advanced training. This inter-American educational cooperation begun by Tireman has continued at the university.[51]

By 1950 Tireman's writing and public speeches declined abruptly. The long-term effects of heart disease and not-yet-diagnosed chronic leukemia had sapped his strength. Though he continued to serve as an educational consultant to foreign countries, it was clear that his drive and enthusiasm had been diminished.[52]

In 1958, in a move to regain his vigor, he and Pearl spent

a year in Hawaii where he was a guest professor. Despite temporary improvement in his physical condition Tireman was ordered to bed by his physician soon after his return to Albuquerque. Unable to teach his classes or supervise his student-teachers, he nonetheless wrote long memoranda to the substitute instructors suggesting how the classes might be run.

On the morning of October 25, 1959, Pearl fixed breakfast. When she returned to the bedroom to wake Loyd she found he had died. The brave, energetic, difficult, and farseeing educator had succumbed to heart disease and leukemia.[53]

6

An Assessment of Tireman's Work

Finding references to Tireman in the history of American education is not an easy task. He and his work are almost totally neglected. Reading textbooks and histories of education fail to mention him, San José, or Nambé.

An evaluation of Tireman and his work will have to deal with the related question of why has this man and his efforts been forgotten? Is the story of Tireman, San José, and Nambé a minor "backwoods" episode in the history of American education, or have historians and educators failed to recognize the value of Tireman's work? If the latter is the case, then the record must be set straight and the reasons for the failure to investigate practical educational reforms must be explored.

The previous chapters established the significance of Tireman as an innovative educator in bilingual and bicultural education at a time when there was little concern with cultural relations in the nation or in the Southwest. Reasons for the neglect of Tireman's work become more difficult to understand when it is realized that programs he developed dealt successfully with some social and educational problems that still trouble the modern world.

In the programs he directed, Tireman explored the use of the active curriculum, language experience, and learning materials relevant to the experience of Hispanic children. The curriculum developed at San José and Nambé clearly foreshadowed modern whole language methods and anticipated contemporary concerns with relevance and "vital interest in content."[1]

Before Goodlad, Coleman and the Holmes Committee, he recognized the difficulties of educational change. At San José he attempted to deal with reform at several different levels using research, classroom methods, teacher training, and follow-up support for cadet teachers who returned to their schools. The contemporary teacher education reform efforts of the Holmes Committee would profit from a study of the cooperation between the university, the San José Demonstration School, and the Key Schools.

In the modern world amicable school-community relations remain one of the most difficult goals to attain. Tireman made great efforts to obtain the trust of the communities in which he worked. Needs assessments were done to secure a sense of what the community felt were problems. Curriculum was conceived of broadly enough to include cultural concerns as well as problems that affected the entire community. The frustrating experiences at the Nambé Community School indicate that this aspect of Tireman's work was probably least successful.

At Nambé he became one of the few educators to implement the methods of social reconstruction in a Hispanic community. In this village struggling under the dead weight of the Depression, the ideas of Counts, Dewey, and Ward were applied to alleviate the real problems of real people.

Tireman and his work are worthy of note, and so the next logical question is why has he not received the attention he deserves? The record of human endeavors is rarely logical. In ways that are sometimes inexplicable, one man is forgotten while another becomes a celebrity. It is unfortunate that scholarly investigations as well as popular records sometimes neglect worthwhile human accomplishments. But there is something to learn from collective forgetfulness, or "amnesia" as Alvin Gouldner terms it.[2] Forgetting is not haphazard; neglect may be unplanned but it is rarely accidental. Examination of the apparent reasons why Tireman's accomplishments have been overlooked can teach us something important about the way that what we call knowledge is formed, about how the historical record is written.

There are some reasons for the neglect that Tireman himself created or at least contributed to. While these reasons are not sufficient explanations, they still contribute to an understanding of the elements that influence the process of forgetting. Tireman did not write well, and although he published many books and articles, the writings he produced did not come easily. His prose carries the mark of the man: it is typically plain and to the point, there is little of the artistry of a stylist. His writing was not developed around a central theory or philosophy. He was not a theoretician like Dewey, a popularizer as was Harold Rugg, or a standard-bearer of a cause as was George Counts.

A series of unfortunate accidents negatively affected Tireman's career. Zimmerman's sudden death in 1942 removed an important source of support for Tireman's experimental educational efforts. Earlier his survey of European bilingual education had been ruined by the Depression. His early return from Europe probably weakened his standing with the GEB. When the GEB revised its grant policies and retired Favrot,

Tireman's main contact person at the foundation, future funding was effectively ended.

Most disappointing of all, Tireman did not enjoy a vigorous, healthy, and long old age during which he could have brought his ideas and programs to the attention of his fellow educators. By 1950 or so, when illness affected his vigor, Tireman had been in New Mexico twenty-three years and his effective work years were finished.[3] At that time he was only fifty-four, and had he two or three more decades in which to work (as did his more fortunate colleagues Counts, and Dewey) he might be better known.

But physical misfortune and sheer bad luck ought not to hide continuing and fundamental factors that may have been responsible for Tireman's lack of fame or national note. These deeper influences have to do with the complexities of cultural differences and cultural politics as well as the occupational self-imge of educators. He tried to address problems that, at that time, did not attract the national attention of the American public or educators. The economic collapse of 1929 brought to the surface the widespread and barely submerged vein of nativism in the American mentality. Bilingual education must have seemed to many Americans an extravagance at best; at worst it was a waste of scarce tax money on something that was vaguely un-American. Such education was a violation of the "Melting Pot" image that dominated the popular mind, provided political campaign promises, and defined educational goals. It was hard for educators and politicians, it seems, to generate much enthusiasm for the plight of "backwoods" Hispanics when millions were unemployed and starving in the cities to the north. Indeed, there were many (and the situation has not changed today) throughout the rest of the nation who were ignorant of the very existence of the state of New Mexico and its special problems and needs.

In the 1940s, with the advent of World War II, some degree of prosperity returned to the nation to fuel New Deal social and educational programs. But these developments had uneven benefits for Tireman and education in New Mexico. There were many New Deal programs to aid the program at Nambé, but at the national level there was still little interest in cross-cultural concerns. As it so often does in times of stress and external threat, nativism and actions seen as necessary for survival (such as the internment of Japanese-Americans in California) interfered with cultural understanding.

In short, it seems that Tireman attempted to address his fellow Anglos at a time when they could not or did not want to listen. Viewed narrowly the educational experiments he directed took place in rural settings. America's attention was directed toward big cities, industrial growth, and efficient use of tax monies. Conventional wisdom held that rural settings were of little importance compared to cities. In education the primary concern was with consolidating rural schools into larger, more efficient units.

At the same time, he probably was seen by the burgeoning Hispanic political and cultural movements as an outsider who was trying to tell them things it was hard for them to hear and accept. It was probably difficult for Hispanic activists to acknowledge an Anglo (particularly one not noted for diplomacy) as an educational leader and innovator. Hence, Professor George I. Sánchez, a former New Mexican and an educator whose path had crossed that of Tireman many times, gained attention and fame writing about and arguing for reforms that echoed Tireman's. All of this occurred while the original reformer, Tireman, and his reform programs passed from the collective awareness.[4]

These specific reasons for the failure of modern education to take note of Loyd S. Tireman no doubt explain the immediate, precipitating factors. Taken another way, these reasons are perhaps symptoms of other, more basic pressures that partly explain the reciprocal historical processes of remembering and forgetting.

Despite the recognition that progressive reform in education is usually seen by historians as a national movement, writing about it often focuses on eastern institutions and experiences. Teachers College, Columbia University was the fountain of reformist thought from the turn of the century to the beginning of the Second World War. Dewey, Counts, and Rugg supplied the ideas and defined the abstract goals of the movement. Thorndike and his colleagues provided the methods and rationale for the scientific study of the psychology of the learner and child. Lesser known but still influential professors fanned out across the nation, including professional visits to New Mexico from their headquarters in Morningside Heights, to spread the dual message of child-centered education and quantitative research into how children learned.

So the New York college deserves its preeminent status as promoter of progressivism and producer of the main ideas that fueled educational reform in the first half of the twentieth century. Both funds and foresight joined to make the Teachers College archives rich and fortuitous repositories of a major version of the history of progressivism. The educational historian must be thankful for the resources available there.

Both availability of materials and habitual focus of treatment conspire to direct attention to Teachers College and the East when progressivism is chronicled. Detailed treatment of other progressive experiments, San José, Nambé, or any other, becomes increasingly difficult because of the habit that directs perception to the East and because historical records are so often treated carelessly and neglected in institutions less well endowed than Teachers College. The tendency to see the progressive reform effort in education as an eastern movement, as opposed to seeing it as a broad tradition affecting the nation, may even result in western caretakers of historical records viewing their collections as marginal or unimportant.

Archival neglect due to insufficient funds or to lack of understanding is related to another peculiarity of the attention of American educational historians and their brethren. Despite the preferred self-image that American educators have as hardheaded pragmatists, as doers, there is a contrasting tendency among educational historians and curriculum specialists to concentrate on the realm of the idea. Certainly theoretical or philosophical systems of thought often preceded and encouraged educational reform and development of programs. But admitting that ideas promote action does not explain why educational historians tend to accent the antecedent and neglect the consequent. Dewey urged that the child and his interests and needs be made the starting point for the new progressive curriculum. In his book *Schools for Tomorrow* the philosopher/educator described school programs that implemented his ideas. Unfortunately, subsequent writers exerted great energy and ingenuity analyzing his philosophy, his abstract ideas, and neglected to examine how those ideas were, or were not, translated into real programs that affected actual children. George Counts's notions of social reconstruction, of using schools to rebuild society, have provided a source of analysis for later historians and philosophers. But investigations of the works of both authors tended to emphasize the abstract ideas and neglect programmatic implementation of their philosophies.[5]

The result of the disproportionate attention to theory is an out-of-balance story of some important parts of the history of education in the first five decades of the present century. It is a story that explores ideas and assumes that the ideas were directly translated into action. It is a story that neglects not only the issue of whether the ideas found translation and trial in real schools, but, if they did find concrete expression, how the ideas were influenced and transformed by their contact with the real world. Seen at both San José and Nambé are the difficulties involved in translating idea and theory into program. Even the best of plans are at the mercy of political, social, and economic forces beyond anyone's control.

Hence the record of progressivism is comparatively long on ideas and short on the record of the implementation of these ideas.[6] Comparable to the analysis of progressivist ideas, there is no detailed record of how the application of those ideas was influenced by urban or rural settings, by large schools with big enrollments, or the opposite, and the influence of political arrangements (strong or weak, state or county control in contrast to private schools). We know very little, despite current interest in cultural influences on learning, about how progressivism was translated into programs for the education of minorities. Were the problems of progressive programs in the state-supported, segregated black schools in the Southeast similar to those experienced by Tireman and his colleagues at Nambé? These questions, as important as they are, remain largely unanswered.

Concentration on ideas rather than programs means that San José and Nambé, and probably other local programs as well, have been neglected. Even worse, the work of energetic, innovative people is overlooked or, when noticed, seen as a quaint, mildly interesting regional incident. The predominantly eastern focus in charting the history of progressivism leaves out much that is important.

Contemporary education might learn a lot from close study of local educational experiments in general. The findings of the 1966 investigation of racial opportunity in public schools,

An Assessment 113

the Coleman Report, surprised educators and political liberals alike. After the initial shock at finding that variations in the "quality" of schools apparently did not explain variations in the school achievement of black youngsters wore off, the attempt to explain the findings began. The interpretation of the Coleman Report data might benefit from a close look at San José and Nambé.

In his analysis of the Coleman Report and Jencks's reinterpretation of the Coleman data, Christopher Hurn argues for a kind of deviant case analysis of individual schools:[7]

> large-scale survey research on the effects of schooling tells us nothing directly about highly unusual schools that may have profoundly different effects on students than the great majority of schools. . . . If these rare schools differed from other schools in their social organization, teaching styles, or methods of evaluation, these features could in principle be adopted by other schools. Research on school effects tells us about the effects of the great majority of schools, but it says nothing about the theoretical limits of schooling—about the potential effects of very different kinds of schools.[8]

The search for "rare schools" might be conducted temporally as well as geographically. A close study of experimental schools such as San José and Nambé might reveal some of the theoretically wide variations in school organization and teaching methods that may influence student achievement. The Tireman-inspired schools might help present analysts know what to look for, might aid experimenters in their search for valid operational definitions.

The selective and segmental nature of American educational history neglects that which is possibly evolutionary. In repeated attempts to make teacher preparation more rigorous and relevant, American educators have resorted to special student experiences in controlled school settings. An important and appropriate question for students of American education is: what is the connection between the demonstration schools of the 1920s and 1930s, student teaching today, and the growing number of "professional development schools" inspired by the Holmes Report?[9] Might not the Key Schools of the 1930s hold some important lessons for modern reforms in teacher training?

There is a final perplexity involved in trying to explain why things are forgotten in the history of education in the United States. In the decades of the twentieth century before World War II, schooling was being transformed from a small, local, and largely rural affair into a larger, more standardized effort. The mode of schooling that had been characteristic of much of the American experience was quickly falling before the arguments of scientific management, the "unassailable" logic of financial efficiency, and consolidation. These facts are well known and well researched.

What is not clear, what has not been investigated very deeply or widely, is how these changes affected the people involved. How did people respond to having their children bussed away from the home to school? How did the children respond to it? What role does such moving of children about have in explaining the typically lower achievement rates of children from rural areas? Until recently the literature discussing school consolidation has been uncritical and largely supportive. Such discussions almost always cite evidence of the weak and inept teaching, lack of textbooks and facilities in one-room rural schools. Some of the small schools were not good places to learn and were best replaced. Yet, some small schools were better than others and provided variety of experience. There surely were inventive, imaginative, and hardy women in those distant and lonely schools who explored the "theoretical limits of schooling." The perplexity arises from the fact that educators and historians have neglected these rich sources of research: the history of education is missing some important chapters.[10]

The neglect, perhaps, is not the result of a haphazard approach. Classrooms are bustling, confusing places in which the flood of stimuli at any one time is enough to daunt most people. Imposing cause-effect rationality of quantitative research is a difficult task. Establishing and describing a relationship between a method of teaching, for instance, and an achievement outcome is a difficult task at best. Designating an outcome as due to a large programmatic change—from a traditional Anglo curriculum to a culturally relevant Hispanic one—is as often the result of hope and wish, as it is due to replicable empirical findings.

Responding to critics of schools who want to see the most "bang for the buck," that is, an efficient return on funds invested, educators are faced with a truly intimidating task of charting something called progress. It seems that faced with a task that is probably impossible in any terms that make sense in the development of human beings, educators unconsciously resort to a desperate and probably unconscious deception. This subterfuge may take the form of "discoveries" or fads.

The claims for a discovery in education—a new teaching method, a way to organize a classroom, a new textbook, or the use of electronic gadgetry—initially rest on arguments of plausibility. Because of the complexity of the classroom enterprise, quantitative research support is likely to be indirect, even marginal to the main argument.

The discovery gives the appearance of progress, the new method that will improve student achievement. With much ballyhoo and discussions of what is promised by the innovation, the critics are "answered" seemingly irrefutably by the discovery. There may be some evidence of change but that could be the result of experimenter or Hawthorne effect. The trumpeted discovery, the solution to the problem used by the critics against public education, usually fades from attention as the popular perception, fickle at best, focuses on some other problem that needs "solving."

While there are differences in the discoveries of different epochs, sometimes they are in vocabulary rather than substance. One discovery seldom builds on the preceding in an evolutionary manner. The value of the discovery is primarily based on its public relations impact, its appearance of newness. Therefore the antecedents of the discovery are forgotten. Discussions of the discovery emphasize differences with the past and neglect evolutionary development. Amnesia obscures the similarities and connections between one discovery and the next related one. Modern discussions of "professional development schools" emphasize their seeming uniqueness and pay little attention to past experiments with teacher training. Amnesia obscures, but it also allows the next refurbishing of an old idea to be trumpeted as a new discovery, an innovation. Forgetting allows a way to dust off and reuse an old idea to counter critics and create at least the illusion of progress. Forgetting helps educators "protect" themselves from critics and, in the process, fosters a canon or dogma that explores some ideas and neglects others. The canon neglects the practical as well, and assumes idea and application flow readily one from the other. Discoveries are seen as discoveries and innovations because we have chosen to remain blind to certain questions.

In reforming the education of Hispanic rural children Loyd Tireman saw a rare opportunity, and he spent his life in pursuit of that opportunity. To Tireman, the stammering, stumbling efforts of a youngster bent over his reader were more important, more valuable to individual and human progress, than theories developed in universities or debates in a legislature. Throughout his life he remained captivated by the problems experienced by Hispanic children learning how to read. He was convinced that most of the difficulties experienced by the children and their teachers could be alleviated by changes in professional training. Relevant and rigorous training complemented by lifelong professional education would help teachers lead Hispanic children to successful reading. The resulting mastery of English would, in turn, be the key that would lead the children to happy and successful lives.

Tireman had the courage to act on his convictions. San José and Nambé School provided rare opportunities to demonstrate his beliefs on school reform. That his life was spent in putting his ideas into action rather than explicating them does not make them less valuable. Loyd Tireman and his dedication to teaching children deserve to be remembered. He ought not to be forgotten.

Appendix
The Mesaland Series

Carolyn Babione

Loyd Tireman, assigned to the Inter-American Educational Bilingual Project during World War II, struggled with loneliness as his assignments took him by train back and forth across the country, away from his two young daughters.[1] It was during this time that Tireman conceived the idea that became the Mesaland Series, "a child's library of the wild life of the mesa."[2] The result was seven small, unpretentious books for young children published by the University of New Mexico Press from 1943 through 1949.

The Mesaland series portrays the hardships, fears, and adversities of wildlife. Life and habitat are vividly described, with the eye of a keen observer of wild creatures in their free state. The animals are scientifically true to their species, personalized with names that indicate the animals' qualities or physical characteristics, as well as human attributes of thought and speech. Each book has a leading figure, in whom one's interest is enlisted. The Mesaland stories are all set in the Southwest.

The first half of the twentieth century was "the golden age" of childhood and children's literature.³ The period experienced significant technological advances in printing, greater importance given to children's literature as an adjunct to modern education, and widespread acceptance of children's literature within the literary world.⁴ The era encouraged experimentation in the types of children's books published as well as new and exciting illustrating techniques.⁵ This vitality also resulted in an extraordinary array of good animal stories published for young people from the 1920s through the 1940s.⁶

Children's books rapidly became profitable "big business" during these years. Publishing involved mass production at small cost, with selling outlets not only in book shops but in ten-cent and variety stores, drug stores, and even chain grocery stores.⁷ Children's book sales climbed from twelve million in 1919 to forty million in 1943.⁸ It was amazing that while the country struggled with two tragic wars, and worldwide depression in the years between, that "this segment of human culture—writing and illustrating for children—should come to blossom, and bear such lasting fruit."⁹

The tragedy in international affairs perhaps turned authors' attention to their own land, creating a body of regional literature that had not existed previously.¹⁰ This know-your-own-land movement had focused attention on regional concerns of soil and wildlife conservation as well. The state game warden in New Mexico appealed repeatedly to New Mexico teachers for curriculum that would include wildlife conservation.¹¹ The habits of animals and their place in the balance of nature played a substantial role in the Nambé Community School curriculum directed by Tireman from 1937–1942.¹²

DeHuff judged Tireman's first children's book, *Baby Jack and Jumping Jack Rabbit* (1943), as providing a much needed addition to children's literature of the Southwest.¹³ Her assessment was followed by other commendable reviews. It was highlighted in the *New York Herald Tribune Weekly Book Review* with such favorable phrases as, "off to a fine start," "plenty of drama such as they [children] love," "especially pleased by the rapidity with which each one [story] reaches a satisfactory conclusion," and "drama that Mother Goose might respect."[14] Recognition and favorable reviews quite possibly accounted for the fact that the first book in the series was printed at least three times in 1943 by the University of New Mexico Press.

As Tireman published his second book, *Hop-A-Long* (1944), the war quotas on the weight and quantity of paper supplied to bookmakers had already tightened competition and created problems with reprinting.[15] The number of new titles in children's library collections decreased one-fifth from 1942 to 1943, and the first quarter of 1944 showed a drop of 7 percent below 1943.[16]

Humans in the Mesaland series are, quite naturally, the ranchers and their families who share the mesa with the animals. The Mesaland animals are constantly in danger from the shortsightedness of man. In "The Nest Is Ruined" in the third book in the series (*Dumbee* 1945), two young boys, José and Paul, start a fire to smoke out bees from inside a small cave because they are hungry for honey. When Queen-Mother bee apprehends the seriousness of what the boys are up to, she summons the young bees to follow her. The home fills with smoke and those not obeying are scorched by the fire and die. Dumbee returns, frightened and saddened by the loss. The boys show little remorse as they believe bees are too stupid to know anything.

Queen-Mother assures Dumbee and the young reader that one must rebuild after devastation, a fitting analogy for the order of business necessary following war. Despite this cruel event, Dumbee goes on with his life, taking from the harsh environment all the enjoyment it has to offer. The following story finds Dumbee off on a playful adventure, making up poems as he buzzes across the mesa, discovering blue honey, which turns out to be a can of blue jam.

Man is not the only formidable enemy on the mesa. The animals prey on one another. Tireman's stories teach children, in a straightforward manner, of the precariousness of predatory life in the wild. The tragedies that Tireman's small animals face are rooted in the basic fears of young children—loneliness, rejection, pain, and loss.[17] *Cocky* (1946), a roadrunner, is described as "the strangest looking and fastest bird the animals had ever seen."[18] Tireman shows that roadrunners are most vulnerable when young. Cocky leaves the nest unguarded for a short time and returns too late. "Cocky came in sight just as the hawk was rising from the nest with the little road runner in his claws." Mrs. Road Runner returns to find Cocky, heavy-hearted, sitting on the edge of the empty nest. They console themselves that another egg will hatch in a few days.

Cocky received some of the best reviews of the series. Becker concluded, "the little book stands out in the oversupplied department of 'little animal' books." A reviewer in the *Library Journal* found the book to be a "very unusual item, highly recommended." Jordan found that the book showed a definite sense of the desert with its characteristic animals and plants.[19]

Big Fat (1947), the fifth book of the Mesaland series, centers on prairie dogs who live on the mesa. In this volume Tireman sought to provide some scientific information as well as to provide humorous incidents occurring as the young animals explore their surroundings.[20] Big Fat scampers for shelter from a rainstorm only to find himself stuck in the opening of a den that is too small for him. In his attempts to free himself, Big Fat kicks his companion, Little Ugly, into the mud. Then Little Ugly unintentionally bits Big Fat's tail as he tries to pull him out. Big Fat, with a squeal of pain and rage, squeezes back out of the hole and falls on top of Little Ugly. Tempers flare and friendship is threatened as they quarrel. However, as the sun reappears, friendship is rediscovered and the little animals laugh about the day's events.

Lessons are learned by children through the lives of young animals in such an entertaining and often humorous manner that they are not perceived as preaching. Even though elements of tragedy are apparent in every book, many of the Mesaland stories are so light-hearted that the books are often viewed as little more than humor. *New Mexico Magazine* critiqued *Big Fat* as the story of a prairie dog with a king-sized tummy and a penchant for getting into trouble.[21]

Children learn in *Three Toes* (1949) that the coyote's enemy is man. "How the Coyote Got the Name of Three Toes" portrays the coyote not only as the enemy to the small wildlife down in the arroyos but to the ranchers' farm animals as well. When Three Toes gets caught in a metal trip, he bravely leaves behind three toes that he has chewed off in order to escape. Tireman depicts this gruesome situation in a straightforward, objective manner. To the coyote the matter is summed up in the following manner: "I'm free . . . and a few toes less are nothing."

Children find their own image in the manner in which animals meet adversity. The conflicts of the animals become the child's conflicts. Well-written stories using tragedy create an avenue for heroes to find a solution through their own enlarged or newly discovered capacities.[22] Sometimes the Mesaland animals escape a tragic ending through their brave or cunning ways. Other Mesaland animals perish and a light-hearted story follows to assure the young reader that the other animals have survived the tragedy to continue to enjoy life.

Evelyn Yrisarri helped Tireman adapt the stories for young readers. Although little information could be located on her, the bookcover for *Baby Jack and Jumping Jack Rabbit* states that she was a member of the National Story Tellers' League of Washington, D.C., and a professional storyteller for thirteen years.[23] The manner in which the stories were adapted for young children has been considered by some as a weak component of the Mesaland books. DeHuff's critique of *Cocky* states: "Dr. Tireman has done a good job for elders in the description of the fight between the roadrunner and a rattlesnake, but the details will confuse small children." DeHuff continued, "Too, the text is filled with phrases difficult for children and even stilted for adults, such as, 'with his crest stiffly erected,' 'the protecting color of feathers,' 'gulps of satisfaction.'" *Dumbee* uses vocabulary that would be difficult for youngsters, such as: "beguile," "belligerent," "begrudge," and "bequest." However, Whitney in a critique of *Hop-A-Long* (1944) for the *Chicago Sun Book Week* states, "Evelyn Yrisarri has adapted his [Tireman's] stories skillfully to entertain and inform a young audience."[24] Children's librarian, Williams, found the print and language used in *Cocky* as "just right for fourth graders."[25]

Ralph Douglass, the illustrator for the Mesaland series, was also on the faculty at the University of New Mexico during the 1940s when the stories were written. Health problems had brought Douglass, formerly an acclaimed political cartoonist with the *Chicago Daily News*, to Albuquerque where "a colleague, Loyd Tireman, approached me about illustrating some little stories he was writing about mesa animals."[26]

The fact that Tireman chose a cartoonist to illustrate his books has importance. The sensationalism of comics posed a significant threat to children's literature during the 1940s with the ever increasing popularity of the often strange super heroes.[27] Children's writers were aware of this competition and set out to make books that would compete with the comics as the artist attained a place of equal importance with the writer.[28]

The illustrations in the Mesaland series consistently received good reviews. Critiques often noted the cartoon-like quality of the illustrations. DeHuff began her critique of *Cocky* with, "Ralph Douglass continues to make delightful drawings for the series of books for children about New Mexican animals," and it is illustrated with a "delightful cartoon touch." "Children who like 'funnies' will love *Cocky*."[29] "Ralph Douglas [sic] on a still page can make more animated goings on than Disney on a screen."[30]

Realistic illustrations of the animals add to the attractiveness and appeal of Douglass's work with the Mesaland books. Douglass utilizes wonderful changes in facial and body expressions of the small animals to show emotions such as fright, contentment, and excitement. "Thoroughly enchanting tale of Cocky, the roadrunner, illustrated by Ralph Douglass with verve and hilarious impudence which children should love," one reviewer concluded.[31] *New Mexico Magazine*'s critique of *Big Fat* judges that "the little folks will like this story of his fun and troubles, and the colorful illustrations by Ralph Douglass alone are worth the price."[32]

Hodges's critique of the illustrations in *Quills* (1948) states that they are "striking" and give "variety and dash" to the story.[33] To the very end of the series Ralph Douglass received favorable reviews. "Striking posterlike effect in two colors gives a vivid feeling for the desert of the Southwest and the whole format of the book [*Three Toes*] is beautiful," wrote Newton after concluding that the story content had little plot or characterization.[34]

Though Douglass seldom illustrated the animals with human characterization, the exceptions were for the purpose of adding humor. In *Quills*, the adventuresome little porcupine is illustrated with a red flag waving from his tail, a humorous attempt to warn the young reader of the danger that awaits the approaching coyote. When the jackrabbit Hop-A-Long becomes embarassed, his face is illustrated in red.

Illustrations are used for the purpose of maintaining the child's interest in books during the period when the child learns the mechanics of reading.[35] Each Mesaland book has only two colors and black. These two colors are interchanged every other page throughout each book. The initial use of only two colors was most likely a result of the shortages of printing materials created by the war effort.[36] Douglass showed his high degree of versatility as he used yellow, blue, and black for *Dumbee* and changed the following year to pink, green, and black for *Cocky*. For the young reader, however, this limited use of color can be confusing, as in *Three Toes* the coyote's color changes from beige to charcoal gray and then to white with black head markings within one chapter as a result of the color interchanging every other page.

Most children's literature of the period, including the work of New Mexican writers, was published and distributed through the large east coast companies. These large publishing houses had more extensive advertising and distributing networks than that of a small university press.[37] The University of New Mexico Press was embarking on new territory when it published the Mesaland books, as these were the first young children's books published through the university.[38] Some believed the Mesaland books might encourage other university presses across the country to begin publishing literature for children.[39] The University of New Mexico Press was one of only three university presses publishing children's literature until the 1950s.[40]

In summary, the seven animal books in the Mesaland series were published by Tireman at a time when the market for children's books was expanding. The Mesaland books were in many ways representative of the wide variety of changes and trends in children's literature that occurred in the 1940s: animal stories, scientific accuracy, writing by authors who knew how to make the actual pattern of an animal's life a fascinating experience for the reader, topics involving home rather than abroad, literature that was humorous, light-hearted, and experimentation in printing and illustrating.

The seven Mesaland books received many favorable reviews at the time of publication. Tireman was recognized as a children's author and prominent educator. Douglass was renowned as an illustrator of children's books. Yet the Mesaland series are not now found in children's libraries. The reasons for the lack of long-term popularity of the books are many. Lack of controlled vocabulary in some of the stories may have hindered independent reading of these books by younger children. Published during a time when young children were being sheltered from the harshness of war, some of the stories may have seemed too realistic to the librarians and parents selecting books. The University of New Mexico Press was in the initial stages of publishing books for young children and may have found it difficult to compete with the marketing efforts of the large eastern publishers.

The value of the Mesaland series is that they contributed to the growth and understanding of the developing child. Children who read the books in the decades past learned about age-mate and sibling relationships. They also learned that loneliness, rejection, and loss can be overcome. Children gained a closer kinship with animals of the Southwest and surely developed more tenderness for these animals and a greater urge to learn more about their needs. Children reading animal stories absorb the lore of nature; they learn the harsh lessons of the wilderness and the thoughtlessness and cruelty of humans toward animals.[41] Such books perform the important task of helping children have a firm grasp on the realities and true wonders of the world.[42]

The Mesaland series provided a valuable addition to the children's literature of the 1940s. These seven books were instrumental in helping usher in reading for young children that depicted animals realistically and factually. Many of the short stories in these books are absorbing and would certainly stir the imagination of many of the young children today who are concerned with the conservation and preservation of the wilderness.

Notes

Documents collections and works frequently cited are identified by the following abbreviations:
NMSR   New Mexico School Review
RAC   Rockefeller Archive Collection

Introduction

1. McCullough 1978, 51; Hofstadter 1955, 109.
2. Hofstadter, 10; Goldman 1977, xvii.
3. Fuller 1982, 130.
4. Fuller, 129; Curti 1959, 206. Perhaps more telling than statistics is the childhood memory of the midwestern novelist and essayist Hamlin Garland. Recalling a visit to neighboring Burr Oak School, he wrote that "altogether it possessed something of the dignity of a church." Garland 1917, 122. Garland grew up very near Tireman's birthplace and his beloved uncle, David McClintock, lived in Orchard, Iowa. Garland, 156.
5. Tireman served in the 338th Field Artillery of the 88th Division of the United States Army from July 1917 to January 1919. *Who's Who in American Education*, 1939–1940, vol. 9.
6. In addition to administering the school at Postville, Tireman taught the normal training classes designed to prepare high school students to be elementary schoolteachers. He was also the girls' basketball coach. Beginning at this time a life-

long pattern, Pearl accompanied the team on out-of-town trips as chaperon and to have some time with Loyd. Letter, May 4, 1987, Mrs. Viola Schultz.

7. *The Round Table*, Albuquerque Rotary Club's Weekly News, November 19, 1953.

8. Tireman, through Horn, had some contact with progressive rural educational reforms in Missouri and it is possible these indirect contacts provided the New Mexico educator with germinal ideas for his own reform programs. Ernest Horn had studied with both Professor J. L. Meriam and Marie Turner Harvey when he worked in Missouri. Professor Meriam was the director of the demonstration elementary school of the University of Missouri at Columbia. Mrs. Harvey was a pioneer in training teachers in rural one-room schools in progressive methods. In 1912 she had taken over the Porter School near Kirksville, Missouri, and developed it into a much publicized exemplary rural school. She later developed and taught in the model rural schoolhouse on the campus of the State Normal School (now the Northeast Missouri State Teachers College). Horn had been brought to the University of Iowa to set up that institution's model elementary school. He was known as an empirical investigator in reading and spelling, and was often cited as one of the founders of the science of education. During World War I, Horn was the chairman of the NEA's Committee on Economy of Time in Education. Cremin 1961, 291–92; Dewey and Dewey 1915; Rugg 1936, 190.

9. In the early 1920s a controversy took place that eventually split the progressive movement. Walter Lippman, the journalist, wrote of his fears that the growing reliance among educators and social scientists on standardized tests would dehumanize children. Lewis Terman, the psychologist, argued in reply that tests would identify talent and lead to its more effective development. Strongly influenced by Freudian and

Jungian concerns with healthy emotional development of children, Cobb, Johnson, and Naumberg feared that social needs would submerge creativity and individual needs. Of course, the debate continues. Pragmatic educators like Tireman would have had no difficulty in seeing that the debate was oversimplified and resulted in a false dichotomy. As a practical-minded reformer, he effected a working balance between the two extreme positions. Graham 1967, 31–32; Karier 1967, 235–37.

Chapter 1

1. A search for the reason that Tireman's first name was written with a single "L" was unsuccessful. It may have been family preference or recognition of a traditional Welsh-English spelling. Concerning his last name, in an interview reported in 1935, he indicated that "in England the family name was spelled Tyreman, the prefix 'tyre' meaning servant." Rotary Club 1935.

2. Being interviewed by Tireman must have been a formidable experience for the teachers. Though he had been at the University of New Mexico barely three years, Tireman had earned a widespread reputation as a tough and demanding instructor. A former student who substituted at San José called him a "perfectionist." Marguerite Johnson interview, November 17, 1987. She recalled too that women students taking a science course from him to complete a unit on ecology. Unfortunately their goldfish died and, rather than risk his displeasure and a failing grade, they sneaked into a sorority and dipped replacement fish out of the aquarium there. Another former student, employed as a National Youth Administration aide at San José, called him "impatient" and said Tireman "had an awful reputation" among students. Del Baca Miera inter-

view, November 6, 1989. During interviews with potential employees, the evidence indicates, he typically pressed and confronted people. Those who became flustered or cried he dismissed. Interviewees who responded in kind and refused to be intimidated received more sympathetic treatment. He enjoyed the confrontational style and seemed to cherish those sessions during which a candidate stood up to him.

3. RAC May 8, 1930.
4. Forrest, 1989, 29, 72.
5. NMSR December 1928, 10.
6. Tireman 1930, 626.
7. Ibid.
8. Ibid.
9. It is likely that during the conversations of January 23 to 25, 1930, that the prospects of George I. Sánchez were discussed. Since 1927, Sánchez had been one of the directors of athletics for Bernalillo County. NMSR March 1927, 11. As a student at the university Sánchez had impressed Nanninga and Zimmerman, and that led to a request to Favrot that Sánchez receive a fellowship for advanced study from the GEB. RAC February 3, 1930. In turn Favrot urged Zimmerman to help Sánchez to get in touch with Professor Herschel Manuel and the University of Texas. The advice was taken and thus began the distinguished career in higher education of an educator whose work benefited the Southwest.
10. RAC January 24, 1930.
11. RAC February 6, 1930.
12. RAC February 19, 1930.
13. RAC March 12, 1930.
14. RAC March 17, 1930.
15. RAC February 18, 1930.
16. RAC February 19, 1930.
17. Political pressures as well as busy schedules meant that

Notes to page 22   133

membership of the advisory board changed often. Late in 1930, there appeared a list with a different membership. *Lobo* October 24, 1930. Still later the following names with their occupations were included in a published list:

Mrs. Mary Austin, authoress
Major Herman Baca, disbursement officer
Mr. Kenneth Balcomb, realtor
Dr. H. L. Ballenger, head of the teacher training program at Normal University
Mr. John V. Conway, president of the Spanish-American Normal School
Mrs. Grace Corrigan, state rural school supervisor
U.S. Senator Bronson M. Cutting
Dr. H. W. Distad, head of the teacher training program at New Mexico State Teachers College
Miss Margaret Easterday, Bernalillo County school superintendent
Mr. Gilberto Espinosa, lawyer
Rabbi A. L. Krohn, president of the Bernalillo County board of education
Judge Milton J. Hemick
Mr. Ralph Hernandez, businessman
Mr. Raymond Huff, president of the state board of education
Mrs. Georgia L. Lusk, state superintendent of public instruction
Mr. John Milne, superintendent of Albuquerque school
Mr. Ray J. McCanna, realtor
Dr. S. P. Nanninga, dean of the college of education
Mr. Camilo Padilla, editor of *Sancho Panza* and *Revista Ilustrado*
Mrs. E. A. Perrault, member of the state board of education

Mr. George I. Sánchez, director of the state division of information and statistics

Mr. Brice Sewell, state supervisor of vocational education

Mr. Clyde Tingley, major of Albuquerque

Dr. J. F. Zimmerman, president of the University of New Mexico

(Tireman, Brewster, and Pooler November 1933, 206–8)

The much expanded advisory board illustrates a surer grasp of the political realities, it seems, due to the wider, more varied representation. Mrs. Austin's membership is likely due to her friendship with Senator Cutting. They had met earlier when they both opposed the U.S. Bureau of Customs decision to ban James Joyce's novel *Ulysses* as obscene. They shared a strong and active interest in Spanish colonial arts. Pearce 1979, 167.

18. RAC February 19, 1930.

19. RAC March 4, 1930.

20. The initial request from Zimmerman, Tireman, and others to the GEB for $100,000 is termed an error because of the shocked reaction from Favrot and, later, Jackson Davis. It seems that if Favrot had not been so attracted to the plan for a demonstration school in New Mexico, the whole project might have died. The request for the large sum could have been a misreading of the visitors' statements and GEB policies. It is possible, and plausible in light of later developments, that the large initial request for funds was made as an exceedingly clever maneuver designed to force up the GEB contribution. President Zimmerman was a very skillful negotiator, knew the GEB representatives, and may have taken the lead in the gamble. Professor Tireman does not seem to have had the character or inclination to conceive or carry out such a plan.

21. RAC March 4, 1930.

22. Ibid.
23. RAC March 11, 1930.
24. RAC March 10, 1930.
25. RAC April 2, 1930.
26. U.S. Senator Bronson Cutting was the scion of a wealthy Long Island, New York, family. As a youth he was diagnosed as having tuberculosis and was brought by his mother and sister to Santa Fe for treatment. The therapy was successful and Cutting remained in New Mexico. He became interested in politics and purchased some newspapers to build a political base. In 1927 Governor Dillon appointed Cutting to the unexpired portion of the term of A. A. Jones who had died. Though a Republican in a predominantly Democratic state, Cutting showed he could be successful by the adroit use of his newspapers and by donating money to worthy and well-publicized projects. Using such political tools helped him narrowly defeat Dennis Chavez for a full term in the Senate. Cutting was killed in a plane crash in 1935. Beaupre 1969. In 1929 Cutting had given the university a grant to allow Professor Arthur Campa to do research in the history of the Spanish people in New Mexico. *Lobo* September 20, 1929, 2.
27. RAC April 23, 1930.
28. RAC May 13, 1930.
29. RAC May 17, 1930.
30. RAC May 24, 1930.
31. RAC May 28, 1930.

Chapter 2

1. NMSR December 1930, 1.
2. NMSR January 1931, 1.
3. Though Milne and Tireman differed in some basic ways about educational philosophy this did not make them enemies.

They seemed to admire each other and to share the ultimate goal of good education for all children. Professor Frank Angel recalls hearing the young professor and old administrator arguing vehemently about the place of different policies in the education of children. Frank Angel interview March 26, 1984. Milne strongly supported the efforts that led to the San José demonstration school. Such support reflects a great deal of credit on the character of John Milne.

4. Kamin 1974, 6.
5. Curti 1959, 211–12.
6. In Iowa in Tireman's youth there had been the influential American Protective Association, a leading anti-Catholic and anti-foreigner organization. Higham 1978, 62. When war was declared in 1914, the Iowa Council of Defense was founded to strengthen patriotism and Americanism. "We are going," said the chairman of the Council, "to love every foreigner who really becomes an American, and all the others we are going to ship back home." Higham 1978, 221.
7. The seeming arrogance and paternalism of the administration toward the Mexican Indian masses was probably intensified by the recently ended civil wars. Despite his pioneering efforts in elementary education, José Vasconcelos was still a conservative who felt that the masses needed to be civilized by the introduction of European culture. He told a university audience in 1920 that "we decide the best manner of educating them." He meant that the Ministry of Education would decide what was best for the masses. In another place he likened modern teachers to "noble heroes" of the past and said that they would "redeem" the masses through "work, virtue, and knowledge." Vaughn 1982, 140–41. A few years later, Moises Saenz wrote that the rural school was a "socializing agency." He continued, "above all, the school has to teach these creatures how to live." Vaughn 1982, 1984. Saenz was a strong

force in the development of the Mexican rural school system. When he left the ministry he taught for at least one summer school session at the University of New Mexico.

8. Nancie Gonzalez concluded that racial prejudice was particularly strong in New Mexico from the 1920s into the 1940s. Gonzalez 1969, 204. See also the detailed history of an incident at the University of New Mexico that documents the heightened ethnic tensions in 1933. Gonzales 1985.

9. Gonzales 1985, 245–47, 251–55.

10. Margaret Abreu, former state superintendent of education, taught in San Miguel County in the early 1900s, and wrote of her first experiences with young students. "I greeted them in Spanish, for they knew no English, and I explained that since English was the official language in New Mexico, they would learn that language. . . ." NMSR October 1959, 8.

11. Tireman 1930.

12. Fitzpatrick 1965, 66.

13. Jennie Gonzales was the first teacher at the one-room demonstration school in the mountains at Cedro. In 1932 at the request of Professor Tireman she spoke to the rural section of the state NEA convention. She told of how she had a radio installed in the school soon after she moved there. Only one of the children had ever heard a radio before. That her visions of the relationship between school and community were similar to those held by the San José director is clear from the following passages from her address.

Thus every red-blooded teacher aspires to make her school the center of the community's life. She must be able to draw from her community all that it can contribute toward a better understanding between home and school. . . . May I leave this one thought with you? It does not avail you anything to try to teach the three R's as something separate from the every day life of those who compose your school. The wise teacher draws as much from her community as she puts into it. She does not shut herself in and expect the four walls of her school room to contain only her ideas but makes them so elastic that they embrace all the village. (RAC November 2, 1932, 2, 8, 10)

14. Sjoberg 1947, 17. Perhaps representing this attitude is the testimony of an old Hispanic man who said that in his culture the church was the most important institution. "The school is all right but that belongs to the government. It isn't really ours." A. B. Chavez 1948, 97.

15. Sjoberg 1947; Moore 1947.

16. Tireman wrote Favrot a letter in which he quoted the new Bernalillo County school superintendent as saying of Tireman: "This man is director of a project which will do more to bring the Spanish American and the Anglo-American together than any other thing that is being done in the state." His letter went on to suggest that while the new superintendent, Mr. Gonzales, may have had the facts "twisted" it was good to know that others "believe in the undertaking." RAC January 6, 1931.

17. RAC July 1931, 20–21.

18. Tireman 1930.

19. RAC July 1931, 4.

20. Moore 1947, 61.

21. Ann Jones interview, November 18, 1986.

22. Tireman probably remained relatively uninformed about the complex motives of the Mexican ministry of education officials. What stuck in his mind was the effort of local teachers to serve the local populace and to improve their lives. In an interview conducted on March 26, 1984, Professor Frank Angel, distinguished educator, former dean and university pres-

ident, who was a new teacher in a one-room school in northern New Mexico when the San José school began, emphasized many times the influence of the Mexican effort on Tireman.
23. RAC December 3, 1931.
24. RAC October 31, 1932.
25. RAC November 22, 1932.
26. Tireman, Brewster, Pooler 1933, 214.
27. *Ibid.*
28. RAC February 3, 1933.
29. Gonzales 1985, 252.
30. RAC April 20, 1933.
31. RAC October 26, 1933.
32. RAC January 24, 1934.
33. RAC June 27, 1934.
34. *Ibid.*
35. RAC May 27, 1935.
36. Tireman December 1, 1931, 15–17.
37. RAC First Annual Report 1931, 14.
38. Tireman December 1, 1931, 15.
39. RAC First Annual Report 1931, 13.
40. Tireman, Brewster, Pooler 1933, 211.

Chapter 3

1. "Prejudice, partial information, or personal advantage will cause many hasty decisions. As serious and honest students, we must resist such temptations, admit we don't know it all, roll up our sleeves, and go to work on the parts of the problems we can improve. . . . At the present, there is little confidence in the results of mental tests given to Spanish-speaking children." Tireman 1948, 39, 51.
2. RAC January 1932, 12.
3. RAC First Annual Report 1931, 16.

Notes to pages 50–55

    4. RAC First Annual Report 1931, 17–18.
    5. RAC First Annual Report 1931.
    6. RAC First Annual Report 1931, 22.
    7. NMSR October 1932.
    8. NMSR October 1933.
    9. RAC First Annual Report 1931, 18.
    10. RAC The County Extension Program June 1, 1933, 11.
    11. RAC The County Extension Program June 1, 1933, 3.
    12. Materials sent to cadets and others involved in the county extension program included an evaluation questionnaire and the following items:

    Drill cards for vocabulary seatwork
    Beginning reading unit with 17 charts
    Desirable reading activities, a 15-page bulletin
    An announcement of the circulating library of
        professional books
    Seatwork based on holidays, 18 pages
    Permanent reading seatwork (grades 2 and 3) 12 picture
        paragraphs
    Upper grade material, 15 pages
    Silent Reading Test
    Arithmetic Fundamental Time Checks
    Vocabulary
    First Three Hundred Words of Ayers Spelling Scale
    Story of the One-Room School of Organ, New Mexico
        by Mrs. Merrie Lou Hilton, 20 pages (sent to cadets in
        one-room schools)
    South American Teaching Unit and Test (24 pages)
    Teacher's Check List by Harlan Sininger
    Supplementary Stories for Surprise Stories

    13. RAC Preliminary Report of the First Four Years May 27, 1935, 12.

14. RAC February 15, 1935.
15. RAC March 6, 1935. The GEB and the Julius Rosenwald Fund in Chicago had a history of cooperation. For example, after graduate work in Texas with Professor Manuel, George I. Sánchez received a Rosenwald grant to write a book on education in Mexico. George I. Sánchez 1936.
16. RAC January 31, 1935.
17. As part of the plan to reorganize the GEB and control expenses, in 1937 Dr. Albert R. Mann, former dean of the agricultural college at Cornell was brought in as vice-president in charge of southern education. Economy measures were soon taken and Dr. Mann closed the offices in Richmond, Virginia bringing Jackson Davis and Leo Favrot to New York. Davis remained with the GEB until his retirement in 1947. Leo Favrot retired from the GEB in 1939. Fosdick and Pringle 1962, 267–68.
18. Fosdick 1962, 266–69.
19. RAC May 10, 1935.
20. RAC January 31, 1935.
21. RAC January 21, 1936.
22. RAC February 25, 1936.
23. NMSR September 1936.
24. NMSR September 1936, 6.
25. NMSR November 1937, 14–15.
26. Pamphlets, teaching units, and general aids that came from the curriculum laboratory are as follows, with the date of issue:
1937 Handwriting Instruction
1937 Annotated Bibliography of Professional Magazines
1937 Materials of Instruction, Manual and Buying Guide, Number One
1938 Materials of Instruction, Activities for the Non-Recitation Periods, Number Two

1938 Materials of Instruction, Sources of Free and Inexpensive Materials, Number Three
1938 Suggestions for the Reorganization of the Social Studies Program in the State of New Mexico
1938 Social Science Program for New Mexico
1938 Conservation of Land and Water, A Teaching Unit
1938 The Teacher in a Modern School
1939 Travel by Bus, Second Grade Level
1939 Suggested Daily Program for a One-Room School

27. RAC January 26, 1937.

28. There is no readily apparent reason to think that the reason stated for the ending of San José by Nanninga and Tireman was masking any deeper reasons. By the spring of 1937 Tireman had spent seven exhausting years developing and directing the San José experiment. It seems that his patience more than his energy was exhausted and it must have been particularly frustrating for him to see the carefully planned research ruined by student transiency. Relevant to any understanding of the decision to close the San José school down must be that by this time Harlan Sininger had left to direct the teacher training program at Highlands University. Tireman and Marie Hughes had had an irreparable falling out and she had returned to graduate school on the west coast. The two educators differed in the emphasis they would give bilingual education in a model early childhood program. Tireman advocated heavy emphasis on the native language in such a program. Hughes felt that such emphasis diverted time and energy from learning English. Probably more important than the pedagogical differences though was the difference in personalities. They were both very strong and capable people. Hughes was perhaps oversensitive while Tireman most certainly was abrasive and tended to treat women in a manner that in contemporary terms could be labeled sexist.

29. RAC February 22, 1937.
30. RAC March 23, 1937.
31. RAC April 29, 1937.
32. RAC May 4, 1937.

Chapter 4

1. Interview with Laura Atkinson, September 1987. Interview with Ann Jones, November 1986.
2. RAC November 19, 1931.
3. April 16, 1936. RAC June 22, 1936.
4. Berman 1979, 136–38.
5. Berman 1979, 164. NMSR 1977, 31.
6. Berman 1979, 137.
7. Apodaca 1986, 54–57.
8. Apodaca 1986, 56–57. Berman 1979, 138–40. Some of the motivation for the McCormick's largess was probably due to their desire to preserve an idealized and primitively "pure" Hispanic village life. In this aim they were very much a part of a 1930s intellectual movement that was partially a reaction to urbanization and industrialization. Forrest 1989, 16; 33.
9. "The Great Depression crept into New Mexico so quietly that at first no one knew it was there. Even when officials became aware that the state had a severe unemployment problem they thought exclusively of the many transients. . . . Few expected anything to affect the stability of the Hispanic villages." Forrest 1989, 79.
10. Berman 1979, 122–23. Tireman and Watson 1943, 1–2.
11. Forrest 1989, 10–11. Berman 1979, 128.
12. Berman 1979, 128. Tireman and Watson 1943, 3.
13. Berman 1979, 129.
14. Forrest 1989, 11. Tireman and Watson 1943, 68–69.

15. Berman 1979, 131.
16. Tireman and Watson 1943, 10–11.
17. Albion W. Small was a great admirer of the work of L. F. Ward. He was also the founder of the first department of sociology in an American university (University of Chicago, 1893). In 1896, Small addressed the National Education Convention in Buffalo, New York and challenged teachers to use their influence to reform society. George S. Counts was a student of Small's and in 1932 published the enormously influential book, *Dare the Schools Build a New Social Order?* Karier 1967, 118–19. Tyack, Lower, and Hansot 1984, 18–27. See the discussion in: Tireman February 1940, 130–33.
18. Tireman and Watson 1943, 13.
19. Preservation of Hispanic villages and Spanish Colonial Arts had its roots in attitudes that were ambivalent in ways characteristic of the era. Cultural differences might be felt to enrich the nation as long as those differences did not impede the country economically or politically. Mary Austin, Frank Applegate, and others of the Santa Fe circle were committed "to rebuilding the shattered cultures of the Southwest as a legacy to the world." They invested considerable resources and effort in the work. Yet, in another place, Mary Austin argued that Hispanic culture was on a "different level" compared to Anglos, and Hispanic "group-mindedness" did not suit them for life in big cities. Forrest 1989, 16, 33–34, 71. Even George I. Sánchez wrote of Hispanic New Mexicans as continuing "inferior and obsolete practices and beliefs" and of their "cultural inadequacy." Sánchez 1940, 13, 27–29.
20. Tireman and Watson 1943, 15.
21. Tireman and Watson 1943, 16–17.
22. Berman 1979, 149. Apodaca 1986, 80–81.
23. Tireman and Watson 1943, 68. Forrest 1989, 11.
24. Tireman and Watson 1943, 69.

25. Tireman and Watson 1943, 75–76. Maria Casias Vergara Interview September 17, 1987.
26. Tireman and Watson 1943, Chapter 5. Maria Casias Vergara Interview September 17, 1987.
27. Tireman and Watson 1943, 74–76.
28. Tireman and Watson 1943, 79–81.
29. Tireman and Watson 1943, 75.
30. Tireman and Watson 1943, 75–76.
31. Berman 1979, 173.
32. Tireman and Watson 1943, 80.
33. Tireman and Watson 1943, 81.
34. Tireman and Watson 1943, 94. Apodaca 1986, 149–50.

Chapter 5

1. Berman 1979, 160, 176.
2. Tireman and Watson 1943, 94. Berman 1979, 160.
3. Berman 1979, 161, 176, 182.
4. Tireman and Watson 1943, 93, 95.
5. Berman 1979, 142.
6. Forrest 1989, 56.
7. C. Ortiz Diary 1937–38.
8. Forrest 1989, 57–58.
9. F. Angel Diary 1937–38.
10. Forrest 1989, 110–11.
11. Berman 1979, 151. Tireman and Watson 1943, 61.
12. Berman 1979, 154–55.
13. F. Angel Diary 1937–38.
14. Berman 1979, 173.
15. Berman 1979, 175.
16. F. Angel Diary 1937–38. Apodaca 1986, 123.
17. Apodaca 1986, 123–24.

18. Berman 1979, 177–79. Forrest 1989, 63, 80.
19. Tireman and Watson 1943, 97.
20. Berman 1979, 178–79. Tireman and Watson 1943, 97–99.
21. Tireman and Watson 1943, 99.
22. "Just as school was called a car drove up. Our visitor turned out to be Mrs. Gilbert, the County Extension Agent. She organized the Girls 4H Club and she plans to be with us the second and last Thursday of every month." M. Watson Diary 1937–38. This was recorded in October 1937, one month after the Nambé Community School began. Apodaca 1986, 100.
23. M. Watson Diary 1937–38. Apodaca 1986, 136.
24. Tireman 1948, 194–95.
25. Berman 1979, 179. Tireman and Watson 1943, 99.
26. Apodaca 1986, 102. F. Angel Diary 1937–38.
27. Tireman 1939, 79.
28. *Ibid.*
29. *Ibid.*
30. Tireman 1939, 79–80.
31. Apodaca 1986, 129.
32. Berman 1979, 181–82.
33. Berman 1979, 181.
34. Tireman 1948, 198.
35. Berman 1979, 182.
36. Berman 1979, 165–66. F. Angel Diary 1937–38.
37. Apodaca 1986, 105.
38. Apodaca 1986, 173–82.
39. Apodaca 1986, 176.
40. Berman 1979, 145.
41. Apodaca 1986, 175.
42. Apodaca 1986, 177.
43. Margaret Wyss Collins Interview, November 7, 1989.

Tragic coincidences characterize the story of the termination of the Nambé Community School. Lopez may have been a recipient of the same scholarship that aided the career of George I. Sánchez. Lopez attended the University of Chicago, the home of Dewey's Laboratory School, and returned to Nambé to play a key role in ending Tireman's experiment in progressive education.

44. In 1940, two years before the cessation of the Nambé School, George I. Sánchez's book, *Forgotten People*, was published. Later liberal opinion rightly holds *Forgotten People* to be a classic denunciation of neglect and demand for educational reform. But the institutionalized view of the book obscures the fact that it was met with great indignation in northern New Mexico. Hispanics there felt that Sánchez's descriptions of their culture were demeaning. Tragically, Sánchez, whose career Tireman helped protect on at least one crucial occasion (RAC May 9, 11, 16, 1933), authored a book that contributed to the general Hispanic disenchantment with outsiders that ended the Community School.

45. Changing people and institutions is slow work that is also extraordinarily demanding. Continuing work requirements not only physically exhausted the faculty but interfered with their private lives. Intensity of commitment was hard to maintain and, as earlier at San José, faculty left Nambé to continue their own lives. Maria Casias Vergara left to marry. Frank Angel resigned and joined the military when war was declared. Others quit to get jobs closer to home. When the school closed, Mary Watson rejoined the state department of education. She later became the state superintendent of education.

46. Margaret Wyss Collins recalls that there had been great resentment in Nambé about an unspecified incident occurring at a dance in a nearly town. Some girls from the School were

involved in the incident and the School was held responsible. Margaret Wyss Collins Interview, November 13, 1989.

47. According to Mrs. Collins, her husband and Lopez served in the war together. Later the two families remained friends though Lopez and Mrs. Collins would occasionally argue about the Community School. Margaret Wyss Collins Interview, November 7, 1989.

48. Berman 1979, 184. Apodaca 1986, 61–62. Who's Who in American Education, Volumes 9, 11, 13.

49. A short history of the Mesaland Series and an analysis of the separate volumes can be found in the Appendix.

50. Tireman December 1947; January 1948; May 1948; September 1950.

51. Tireman organized and coordinated a seminar for Guatemalan educators at the university in 1954. Report of the Guatemalan Seminar, College of Education, University of New Mexico, October 27 to December 11, 1954. Later the inter-American educational aid efforts were revived and expanded by Frank Angel. Currently the greatly amplified work is directed by Ronald Blood.

52. Phi Delta Kappa, Beta Rho Chapter, 1959–1960 Yearbook 1–5.

53. The official New Mexico state death certificate lists the causes of death as myocardial infarction and chronic leukemia. On the document it is indicated that the leukemia had been first diagnosed two years before death and the heart trouble for six weeks. However, it may be that the onset of both diseases had been gradual and their effects had been slowly debilitating. Tireman's slowly losing battle with these illnesses may have resulted in depression. Therefore it is not unreasonable to assume that both physical and emotional stresses led to the decline in his professional output after 1950.

Chapter 6

1. Chall 1967, 61.
2. Gouldner 1980.
3. A student of Tireman's in the early 1950s remembers that she was disappointed with his teaching of a methods class. He did not provide teaching suggestions or demonstrate an awareness of current instructional methods. She confronted the professor and was told that he taught the theory and not specific methods. The incident probably tells more about Tireman's declining level of vigor than about his philosophy. Interview with S. D. Smith December 8, 1987.
4. Schlossman Summer 1983.
5. Cuban 1984. Zilversmit 1976.
6. Cuban 1984; 1986.
7. Coleman 1966. Jencks 1972.
8. Hurn 1978, 105–51.
9. Holmes Group Executive Board 1986.
10. Sher 1977. Hayes 1948. Kaufman 1984. Weber 1946.

Appendix

1. Homan 1971.
2. Major, Smith and Pearce 1948, 160.
3. Viguers 1953.
4. Viguers 1953; Lystad 1980.
5. Sayers 1944; Viguers 1953.
6. Smith 1963.
7. Viguers 1953.
8. Clark 1944.
9. Sayers 1944, 162.
10. Viguers 1953; NMSR 1940.
11. Barker 1937, 1938a, 1938b.

12. Watson and Angel 1939.
13. DeHuff 1944.
14. Becker 1944, 5.
15. *Library Journal* 1944.
16. Clark 1944.
17. Kingston 1974.
18. The Booklist 1946, 370.
19. James and Brown 1947; Becker 1946, 984; Williams 1946, 984; Jordan 1946.
20. Evans 1947, 150.
21. *New Mexico* 1947, 53.
22. Kingston 1974.
23. DeHuff 1946, 58.
24. Whitney 1945, 11.
25. Williams, 1946, 984.
26. Viguers, Dalphin and Miller 1958, 102.
27. Hogarth 1943; Eichenberg 1944.
28. Viguers 1953.
29. DeHuff 1946, 58.
30. Evans 1947, 150.
31. Williams 1946, 984.
32. New Mexico 1947, 53.
33. Hodges 1948, 1826–27.
34. Newton 1950, 880–81.
35. Viguers 1953.
36. Blake 1943.
37. *Library Journal* 1949.
38. DeHuff 1944.
39. Evans 1947.
40. Johnson 1952.
41. Huck and Young 1961.
42. Adams 1953.

Selected Bibliography

Adams, Bess Porter. *About Books and Children: Historical Survey of Children's Literature.* New York: Henry Holt and Company, 1953.

Apodaca, Rita C. "The Nambé Community School (1937–1942): A Study of a Community-Relevant Curriculum." Ph.D. diss., University of New Mexico, 1986.

Aurner, Clarence R. *History of Education in Iowa.* Iowa City, Iowa: The State Historical Society of Iowa, 1914.

Baker, Ray Stannard. *Native American: The Book of My Youth.* New York: Charles Scribner's Sons, 1941.

Barker, E. S. "The Need for Education in Wildlife Conservation." *New Mexico School Review* 16 (1937): 14–17.

———. "How Can I Help Conserve Wildlife?" *New Mexico Magazine* 16 (1938a): 31.

———. "Educational Program Needed." *New Mexico Magazine* 16 (1938b): 27.

Becker, M. L. "Books for Young People." *New York Herald Tribune Weekly Book Review* (March 19, 1944): 5.

———. "Books for Young People." *New York Herald Tribune Weekly Book Review* (July 26, 1946): 5.

Beaupre, Richard H. "The 1934 Senatorial Election in New Mexico." M.A. thesis, University of New Mexico, 1969.

Berman, Martin L. "Arthurdale, Nambé, and the Developing Community School Model: A Comparative Study." Ph.D. diss., University of New Mexico, 1979.

Blake, E. "How Will Children's Books Look in 1944?" *Library Journal* 68 (1943): 1039.
Bonnifield, Paul. *The Dust Bowl: Men, Dirt, and Depression.* Albuquerque, N.M.: University of New Mexico Press, 1979.
Booth, George C. *Mexico's School-Made Society.* Stanford: Stanford University Press, 1941.
Bright, Robert. *Georgie.* New York: Doubleday, 1944.
Brown, Margaret Wise. *The Little Island.* Garden City, N.Y.: Doubleday Company, 1946.
Cassidy, Ina Sizer. "Art and Artists of New Mexico." *New Mexico* 25 (1947): 26.
Chall, Jeanne S. *Learning to Read: The Great Debate.* New York: McGraw-Hill, 1967.
Chavez, Aristides B. "The Use of the Personal Interview to Study the Subjective Impact of Culture Contacts." Master's Thesis, University of New Mexico, 1948.
Clark, Ann Nolan. *In My Mother's House.* New York: Viking Press, 1941.
Clark, M. M. "Wartime Production and Children's Books." *Library Journal* 69 (1944): 535–36.
Coleman, James S. et al. *Equality of Educational Opportunity.* Washington, D.C.: U.S. Government Printing Office, 1966.
Cowley, Malcolm. *Exile's Return: A Literary Odyssey of the 1920's.* New York: The Viking Press, 1956.
Cremin, Lawrence. *Transformation of the School: Progressivism in American Education.* New York: Alfred A. Knopf, 1961.
Cuban, Larry. *How Teachers Taught: Constancy and Change in American Classrooms, 1890–1980.* New York: Longman, 1984.
Cummings, Richard L. and Donald A. Lemke. *Educational Innovations in Latin America.* Metuchen, N.J.: Scarecrow Press, 1973.
Curti, Merle. *The Social Ideas of American Educators.* Paterson, N.J.: Pageant Books, 1959.

DeHuff, E. W. *Pals*. New York: Mentzer, Bush and Company, 1936.
———. *Hoppity Bunny's Hop*. Caldwell, Idaho: Caxton Printers, 1939.
———. *New Mexico* 22 (1944): 34.
———. *New Mexico* 24 (1946): 58.
Dewey, John and Evelyn Dewey. *Schools of Tomorrow*. New York: E. P. Dutton, 1915.
Dobie, J. F. "Nature; Wildlife; Naturalists" in *Guide to Life and Literature of the Southwest*. Dallas: Southern Methodist University Press, 1952.
Douglass, Ralph. *Calligraphic Lettering*. New York: Watson-Guptill, 1949.
Eichenberg, F. "New Picture Books." *The Horn Book* 20 (1944): 15–24.
Evans, E. "1946 Children's Books." *The Commonweal* 47 (1947): 150.
Fitzpatrick, Mildred G. "Textbooks Used in the Elementary Schools of New Mexico (1846–1964)." Ph.D. diss., University of New Mexico, 1965.
Forrest, Suzanne. *The Preservation of the Village: New Mexico's Hispanics and the New Deal*. Albuquerque: University of New Mexico Press, 1989.
Fosdick, Raymond B. *Adventure in Giving: The Story of the General Education Board*. New York: Harper and Row, 1962.
Fuller, Wayne E. *The Old Country School: The Story of Rural Education in the Middle West*. Chicago: University of Chicago Press, 1982.
Garland, Hamlin. *A Son of the Middle Border*. New York: Grosset and Dunlap, 1917.
Giles, R., D. E. Cook, and D. H. West. *Children's Catalog*. New York: The H. W. Wilson Company, 1946.

Goldman, Eric F. *Rendezvous with Destiny: A History of Modern American Reform.* New York: Vintage Books, 1977.

Gonzales, Phillip B. "A Perfect Furor of Indignation: The Racial Attitude Confrontation of 1933." Ph.D. diss., University of California, Berkeley, 1985.

Gouldner, Alvin W. *The Coming Crisis of Western Sociology.* New York: Basic Books, 1980.

Graham, Patricia Albjerg. *Progressive Education: From Arcady to Academe.* New York: Teachers College Press, 1967.

Hader, Berta and Elmer Hader. *The Big Snow.* New York: Macmillan Company, 1948.

Harrington, M. P., ed. *The Southwest in Children's Books—A Bibliography.* Baton Rouge: Louisiana State University Press, 1952.

Higham, John. *Strangers in the Land: Patterns of American Nativism 1860–1925.* New York: Atheneum, 1978.

Hodges, E. "New Books Appraised: Part II—Children's Books." *Library Journal* 73 (1948): 1826–27.

Hofstadter, Richard. *Academic Freedom in the Age of the College.* New York: Columbia University Press, 1964.

———. *The Age of Reform.* New York: Vintage Books, 1955.

Hogarth, G. A. "Virginia Lee Burton: Creative Artist." *The Horn Book* 19 (1943): 221–27.

Holloway, Jean. *Hamlin Garland: A Biography.* Austin, Texas: University of Texas Press, 1960.

Homan, M. J. "Children's Books by New Mexico Writers." Master's Thesis, University of New Mexico, 1971.

Huck, C. S. and D. A. Young. *Children's Literature in the Elementary School.* New York: Holt, Rinehart and Winston, 1961.

Johnson, S. J. Introduction in M. P. Harrington (ed.). *The Southwest in Children's Books—A Bibliography.* Baton Rouge: Louisiana State University Press, 1952.

Jordan, A. M. "The Booklist." *The Horn Book* 22 (1946): 266.
Kamin, Leon J. *The Science and Politics of I.Q.* New York: John Wiley and Sons, 1974.
Karier, Clarence J. *Man, Society, and Education: A History of American Educational Ideas.* Glenview, Illinois: Scott, Foresman and Co., 1967.
Kingston, C. T. *The Tragic Mode in Children's Literature.* New York: Teachers College Press, 1974.
Library Journal. "Juvenile Editors Give Assurance." 69 (1944): 537–38.
Lingeman, Richard. *Small Town America: A Narrative History, 1620–The Present.* Boston: Houghton Mifflin Co., 1980.
Lystad, Mary. *From Dr. Mather to Dr. Seuss: 200 Years of American Books for Children.* Boston: G. K. Hall and Company, 1980.
Major, M., R. W. Smith, and T. M. Pearce. *Southwest Heritage.* Albuquerque: University of New Mexico Press, 1948.
Major, M. and T. M. Pearce. *Southwest Heritage.* Albuquerque: University of New Mexico Press, 1972.
Meigs, C., ed. *A Critical History of Children's Literature.* New York: Macmillan, 1953.
Metzgar, Walter P. *Academic Freedom in the Age of the University.* New York: Columbia University Press, 1969.
McCullough, James B. *Hamlin Garland.* Boston: Twayne Publishers, 1978.
Moore, Frank C. "San Jose, 1946: A Study in Urbanization." Master's Thesis, University of New Mexico, 1947.
Nasaw, David. *Schooled to Order: A Social History of Public Schooling in the United States.* New York: Oxford University Press, 1979.
New Mexico Magazine. "Southwestern Book Shelf." 25 (1947): 53.

New Mexico School Review. "New Mexico Teachers Authors of Texts in Reading." 19–20 (1940): 16.
Newton, L. "Part II: Children's Books." Library Journal 75 (1950): 880–81.
Pearce, T. M., ed. Literary America, 1903–1934: The Mary Austin Letters. Westport, Conn.: Greenwood Press, 1979.
Peshkin, Alan. Growing Up American: Schooling and the Survival of Community. Chicago: University of Chicago Press, 1978.
Rugg, Harold. American Life and the School Curriculum. Boston: Ginn and Company, 1936.
Sarkissian, A., ed. Children's Authors and Illustrators: An Index to Biographical Dictionaries. Detroit, Michigan: Gale Research Company, 1978.
Sayers, F. C. "Of Memory and Muchness." The Horn Book 20 (1944): 153–63.
Sjoberg, Gideon. "Culture Change as Revealed by a Study of Relief Clients of a Suburban New Mexico Community." Master's Thesis, University of New Mexico, 1947.
Skinner, M. C. "The Picture Book Age: Outstanding Books for Youngest Readers." Library Journal 69 (1944): 861–63.
Smith, D. V. Fifty Years of Children's Books, 1910–1960: Trends, Backgrounds, Influences. Champaign, Illinois: National Council of Teachers of English, 1963.
Stong, Phil D. If School Keeps. New York: Frederick Stokes and Co., 1940.
Strang, M. "New Books Appraised." Library Journal 72 (1947): 1784.
Rugg, Harold. American Life and the School Curriculum. Boston: Ginn and Co., 1936.
Sánchez, George I. Mexico: A Revolution by Education. New York: Viking Press, 1936.

———. *Forgotten People: A Study of New Mexicans*. Albuquerque: University of New Mexico Press, 1940.
Tamblyn, Lewis R. *Rural Education in the United States*. Washington, D.C.: Rural Education Association, 1971.
The Booklist. American Library Association 40 (1944): 360.
The Booklist. American Library Association 42 (1946): 370.
Turner, Frederick Jackson. *The Frontier in American History*. New York: Henry Holt and Co., 1920.
Tyack, David, Robert Lowe, and Elisabeth Hansot. *Public Schools in Hard Times: The Great Depression and Recent Years*. Cambridge: Harvard University Press, 1984.
Vaughan, Mary Kay. *The State, Education, and Social Class in Mexico, 1880–1928*. De Kalb: Northern Illinois University Press, 1982.
Viguers, R. H. "Part Four: 1920–1950, The Golden Age." In C. Meigs, ed., *A Critical History of Children's Literature*. New York: Macmillan, 1953.
———, M. Dalphin, and B. Miller. *Illustrators of Children's Books, 1946–1956*. Boston: The Horn Book, 1958.
Vogel, Albert W. and Martin L. Berman. "The School at Nambé." *New Mexico School Review* 53 (1977): 12–15.
Waggoner, Laura. "San José: A Study in Urbanization." Master's Thesis, University of New Mexico, 1941.
Watson, Mary and Frank Angel. "The Study of the Land and Its Relation to Living." *New Mexico School Review* 19 (1939): 15–17.
Whitney, P. A. *Chicago Sun Book Week* (March 4, 1945): 11.
Williams, G. "New Books Appraised." *Library Journal* 71 (1946): 984.
Zilversmit, Arthur. "The Failure of Progressive Education, 1920–1940." In *Schooling and Society: Studies in the History of Edu-*

cation, edited by Lawrence Stone. Baltimore: Johns Hopkins Press, 1976.

Zintz, Miles V. *Corrective Reading.* Dubuque, Iowa: William C. Brown, 1966.

Tireman's Publications

Tireman, Loyd S. "Value of Marking Hard Spots in Spelling." *University of Iowa Studies in Education* 5, No. 4 (1930).

———. "Reading in the Elementary Schools of New Mexico." *Elementary School Journal* 30 (April 1930): 621–26.

———. "New Mexico Tackles the Problem of the Spanish-Speaking Child." Journal of Education 114 (November 1931): 300–301.

——— and Mary Austin. *Rural Schools of Mexico and Rural Education in New Mexico.* Training School Series, vol. 2, no. 1, University of New Mexico Press, 1931.

———, Newel Dixon, and Vera Cornelius. "Vocabulary Acquisition of Spanish-Speaking Children." *Elementary English Review* 12 (May 1935): 118–19.

———. "New Mexico's Program of Curriculum Development." *Curriculum Journal* 8 (February 1937): 65–66.

——— and Marie Hughes. "Reading Programs for Spanish-Speaking Pupils." *Elementary English Review* 14 (April 1937): 138–40.

——— and V. E. Woods. "Aural and Visual Comprehension of English by Spanish-Speaking Children." *Elementary School Journal* 40 (November 1939): 204–11.

———. "Nambé: A Community School." *Curriculum Journal* 10 (November 1939): 323–24.

———. "Discovery and Use of Community Resources in the Education of Spanish-Speaking Pupils." In *Community Resources in Rural Schools,* 72–85. Washington, D.C.: Department of Rural Education, National Education Association, 1939.

———. "Note on the Influence on the Validity of a Vocabulary Test of the Method of Indicating Responses." *Journal of Educational Psychology* 31 (February 1940): 153–54.

———. "Elementary Curriculum as a Tool for Improving the Community." *Progressive Education* 17 (February 1940): 130–33.

———. "School Problems Created by Homes of Foreign-Speaking Children." *California Journal of Elementary Education* 8 (May 1940): 234–38.

———. Review of *Forgotten People*, by George I. Sánchez. *Curriculum Journal* 12 (February 1941): 91–92.

———. "Teaching Spanish in the Upper Elementary Grades." *Hispania* 24 (May 1941): 217–22.

———. "Bilingual Children." *Review of Educational Research* 11 (June 1941): 340–52.

———. "School Problems Created by Foreign Speaking Children." *Texas Outlook* 26 (November 1942): 19–20.

———. "Teaching Spanish in the High School." *Hispania* 26 (February 1943): 35–40.

——— and Mary Watson. *La Comunidad: Report of the Nambé Community School, 1937–1942.* Albuquerque, N.M.: University of New Mexico Press, 1943.

———. *Baby Jack and the Jumping Jack Rabbit.* Albuquerque, N.M.: University of New Mexico Press, 1943. Mesaland Series.

———. "Bilingual Children." *Review of Educational Research* 14 (June 1944): 273–78.

———. "Rights and Responsibilities." In *Report of Conferences on Professional Relations and Inter-American Education* at The Southwest Texas State Teachers College, San Marcos, Texas, July 1944.

―――. *Hop-A-Long.* Albuquerque: University of New Mexico Press, 1944. Mesaland Series.

―――. "Study of 4th Grade Reading Vocabulary of Native Spanish-Speaking Children." *Elementary School Journal* 46 (December 1945): 223–27.

―――. *Dumbee.* Albuquerque: University of New Mexico Press, 1945. Mesaland Series.

―――. *Cocky.* Albuquerque: University of New Mexico Press, 1946. Mesaland Series.

―――. "Some Aspects of Bolivian Education." *Phi Delta Kappan* 29 (December 1947): 207–8.

―――. *Big Fat.* Albuquerque: University of New Mexico, 1947. Mesaland Series.

―――. "Principles of Supervision Applied in Normal School Reorganization in Bolivia." *Educational Administration and Supervision* 34 (January 1948): 55–59.

―――. *Spanish Vocabulary of 4 Native Spanish-Speaking Pre-First Grade Children.* Publications in Education, no. 2. Albuquerque, N.M.: University of New Mexico Press, 1948.

―――. *Teaching Spanish-Speaking Children.* Albuquerque, N.M.: University of New Mexico Press, 1948.

――― and Mary Watson. *Community School in a Spanish-Speaking Village.* Albuquerque: University of New Mexico Press, 1948.

―――. *Quills.* Albuquerque: University of New Mexico Press, 1948. Mesaland Series.

―――. "Bolivia—The Hermit Nation." *New Mexico School Review* 27 (May 1948): 5, 29.

―――. "Neglect Not the Bright Child." *New Mexico School Review* 28 (October 1948): 6–7.

―――. *Three Toes.* Albuquerque: University of New Mexico Press, 1949. Mesaland Series.

———. "Combating Illiteracy in the Americas." *New Mexico School Review* 30 (September 1950): 13, 27.

———. "Report of Guatemala Seminar, October 27 to December 11, 1954." College of Education, University of New Mexico. Photocopy.

———. "Bilingual Child and His Reading Vocabulary." *Elementary English* 32 (January 1955): 33–35.

———. "Show and Tell." *New Mexico School Review* 35 (May 1956): 19.

——— and Miles Zintz. "Factors Influencing Learning a Second Language." *Education* 81 (January 1961): 310–13.

Index

Adult literacy. See Literacy, adult.
Agriculture, 68–69, 80, 82, 83, 84–88, 89
Arnett, Trevor, 56
Atkinson, Laura, 60, 61
Austin, Mary Hunter, 21, 71, 144n.19

Balling, Marie, 21, 26
Bilingual/Bicultural Education, 7, 9, 36, 39–41, 105, 108, 137n.13, 142n.28; European bilingual programs, 42–43; home language environment, 15; reading survey findings for New Mexico Spanish-speaking children, 15
Bulletin to rural teachers, 53

Casias, Mary, 80, 90
Cedro demonstration school, 52, 137n.13
Coleman, James S., 106

The Coleman Report (1966), 112–13
Community. See School-Community relations.
Community School in a Spanish-Speaking Village [La Communidad], by Tireman and Watson, 70, 88–89, 102
Counts, George S., 71, 106, 107, 110, 111, 144n.17
County Extension Program, 53–54, 140n.12. See also Marie Hughes; See also Key Schools plan.
Cultural colonization, 30
Curriculum laboratory at the University of New Mexico, 60–61
Curriculum revision program, 8, 35, 48–49, 53, 58–59. See also San José Demonstration School innovations.

Cutting, Bronson, 21, 23, 25, 30, 57, 135n.26

Davis, Jackson, 17, 18, 23, 26, 134n.20, 141n.17
Dewey, John, 106, 107, 110

Educational philosophies and national movements; agrarian radicalism, 3, 30; conservative, assimilationist view, 28, 29; nativism, 7, 28, 29, 39–40, 108, 109; populism, 3–4; progressivism, 5, 29–30, 35, 36, 71, 110, 112, 130n.8, 130–31n.9; social reconstructionists, 71; traditionalist educators, 28, 39–40, 70–71
Educational reform, 9, 144n.17. See also Rural educational reform.
Elementary school reading program reform, 15–16
Embree, Edwin R., 56
Emergency Education Act, 83
English language instruction and enrichment, 36, 38, 92–93
Experimental demonstration schools, 113–14, 130n.8

Favrot, Leo, 11, 12, 13, 17, 19, 20, 22, 23, 24, 25, 26, 41, 47, 55, 57, 58, 59, 61, 64, 107, 132n.9, 134n.20, 138n.16, 141n.17
Federal Emergency Relief Administration (FERA), 83
The Forest Service, 89, 97

General Education Board (GEB), 11, 12, 13, 17, 18, 19–20, 22–26, 41, 46, 55, 56–57, 59, 107, 134n.20, 141n.15; discussions with The University of New Mexico, 19; precedent of working through local state officials, 20; requirement of securing local funds, 20; Zimmerman, James Fulton, 17. See also San José Demonstration and Experimental School.
Gilbert, Fabiola C. de Baca, 90, 146n.22
Gonzales, Jennie, 52, 137–38n.13
Goodlad, John I., 106
Gouldner, Alvin, 107
The Great Depression, 23, 40, 68, 79, 80, 88, 100, 106, 107, 108, 143n.9

Health conditions, 69, 70, 73–74
Health education and care, 45, 69, 73, 74–78, 81, 82, 84, 90
Hispanic education, 5, 13, 32–32, 36, 39, 40–41, 43–44, 48–49, 53, 56, 70, 91, 106, 108, 115, 116–17
Hispanic rural life and art, 45–46, 71; preservation of, 71, 143n.8, 144n.19
The Holmes Committee, 106
The Holmes Report, 114
Horn, Ernest, 19, 130n.8
Hughes, Marie, 54, 55, 60, 61, 142n.28
Hurn, Christopher, 113

Indian Pueblo Lands Controversy, 82
Intelligence, achievement, and assessment testing, 29, 34–35, 47

Jencks, 113
Julius Rosenwald Fund of Chicago, 56

Key Schools plan, 53–54, 114. See also County Extension Program.
Krohn, A. L., 22
Kyte, 19

Literacy, adult, 60, 83
Lopez, Frank, 99–100, 148n.47

McCormick, Mr. and Mrs. Cyrus J., 62, 64–67, 71, 74, 75, 87, 97, 143n.8.
Mexican rural experiment. See Tireman.
Milne, John, 17, 21, 24, 25, 27–28, 135–36n.3.
Montoya, Atanasio, 17, 20, 21
Mutual Protective Society of United Workers (SPMDTU), 79, 80

Nambé, 62, 66–70, 79. See also McCormick.
Nambé Community School, 8, 71–73, 79–82, 91–99, 106; agricultural training, 84–88, 94–96; language acquisition and enrichment, 92–94, 95; legal landownership education, 82–83; PTA and SPMDTU, 79–80; reasons for termination, 97–102, 147n.43; San José reading program applied, 92–94; science project, 94–95; state and federal agencies, use of, 83, 88, 90, 91–92; woodworking shop, 89, 96–97
Nanninga, Simon Peter, 16, 55, 61, 62, 64, 66, 142n.28
National Youth Administration (NYA), 89, 97
New Mexico Education Association Conference, 27
The New Mexico Sentinal, 65

Opportunity Room, 35–36, 52
Oral reading method, 32–33
Ortiz, Cordelia, 78, 80
Ortiz y Paiz, Gaspar, 67

Padilla, Camilo, 22
Presentism, 9, 116
Prieto, Rose, 52
Principals: training for small rural schools, 50
Program for Improvement of Instruction, 59, 61. See also Curriculum Revision program.

Racial prejudice, 7, 28–29, 47, 136n.7
Raymond, Ann, 90
Reading education, 15–16, 32, 37–38, 39, 54, 93. See also Tireman: education in New Mexico.
Reform. See Educational reform; Tireman and educational reform.

166   Index

Rockefeller Foundation, 11, 19
Rodgers, H. R., 58, 59
Rugg, Harold, 107, 110
Rural education, 46, 114–15, 130n.8, 136–37n.7. See also rural education reform.
Rural education in New Mexico, 13, 17, 27–28, 31–34, 46, 55. See also Bilingual education; Nambé Community School; San José Demonstration and Experimental School.
Rural education reform, 34, 57–58, 70–71, 101, 106
San José Demonstration and Experimental School, 8, 11–12, 14–16, 18–21, 26, 29, 31, 63–64, 142n.28; advisory board membership, 21–22; catalyst for educational reform, 11, 16, 46; favorable assessments, 16, 18, 55–56; San José village community and social change, 33–34; target of political attacks, 30; termination, 61–62, 64, 142n.28. See also General Education Board; see also Rural education in New Mexico; see also San José Demonstration School innovations.
San José Demonstration School innovations, 8; active curriculum, 35; activity program, 37–39; ESL instruction, 36; formal instruction in Spanish, 39, 40, 43; individualized instruction and attention, 35; language acquisition (experience), 38–39; pre-first class, 36; recreational reading, 37; student-centered, 35; testing program, 34–35. See also Opportunity Room; see also Teacher training program.
Sanchez, George I., 109, 132n.9, 141n.15, 144n.19, 147n.18, 147n.19
Santa Fe Circle, 144n.19
School-Community relations, 7, 9, 33–34, 36, 41, 44–45, 67, 106, 137–38n.13; San José Spanish Colonial Arts and Crafts program, 45–46. See also Curriculum revision program; see also Health education; see also McCormick; see also Nambé Community School.
Sedillo, Mela, 45
Seligman, Arthur, 20, 30–31, 34
Sininger, Harlan, 12, 26, 36, 49, 55, 142n.28
Soil Conservation Service (SCS), 87, 89
Spanish culture. See Hispanic education; Hispanic rural life and art.
Spanish village life. See Hispanic rural life and art.
Teacher training program at San José, 48, 49–51, 52–53, 54, 59–60
Teachers College, Columbia University, 110
Terman, Lewis, 29, 130n.9
Testing. See Intelligence, achievement, and assessment testing.

Tingley, Clyde, 22
Tireman, Loyd, 3–9, 11–12, 27, 28–29, 63–64; agricultural training at Nambé, 84–88; bilingual/bicultural education, concern with, 40, 41, 105, 116–17; *La Communidad*, 102; cultural influences, 3–4, 8; education in New Mexico, 11, 13–14, 15; educational philosophy, 5–6, 8, 30, 37, 71–72, 95–96; educational reform, 5, 8, 11–12, 16, 27, 47–48, 58, 64, 106; European tour to observe national bilingual programs, 41–43, 107; Garretson, Pearl, 4, 102, 129–30n.6; health, 102–3, 108, 148n.53, 149n.3; historical neglect of, 3, 8, 105, 107–10; Latin American education, 102, 148n.51; Mesaland series, 102, 119–28; Mexican rural experiment, 30, 40, 45, 48, 136–37n.7, 138–39n.22; Milne, John, controversy with, 27–28; New Mexico Education Association Conference, 27; personal interview technique, 74, 131–32n.2; reading program goals, 37. *See also* Favrot, Leo; Nanninga, Simon Peter; Sininger, Harlan; Zimmerman, James Fulton; *see also* Nambé Community School; *see also* San José Demonstration and Experimental School; *see also* San José Demonstration School innovations.
Tormey, 55–56

Vergara, Maria Casias, 74, 147n.45

Ward, L. F., 71, 106, 144n.17
Watson, Mary, 60, 70, 78, 80, 81, 84, 89, 90, 91, 102, 147n.45
Whole language methods, 106
Works Progress Administration (WPA), 83, 89

Zimmerman, James Fulton, 16, 17, 18, 20, 21, 22, 23, 24, 25, 26, 55, 57, 62, 64, 66, 132n.9, 134n.20

www.ingramcontent.com/pod-product-compliance
Lightning Source LLC
Chambersburg PA
CBHW022103160426
43198CB00008B/338